Daily
Declarations
of Faith
FOR MEN

BroadStreet
PUBLISHING

BroadStreet Publishing® Group, LLC
Savage, Minnesota, USA
BroadStreetPublishing.com

Daily Declarations of Faith for Men

Copyright © 2021 Joan Hunter
978-1-4245-6193-3 (faux)
978-1-4245-6194-0 (e-book)

Disclaimer: This book is a resource for daily encouragement, hope, and prayer because we believe that Jesus Christ's "divine power has given to us all things that pertain to life and godliness" (2 Peter 1:3). The author and publisher do not claim to treat or diagnose any condition and are not responsible for results from these declarations. The information in this book is not a substitute for professional advice or treatment.

Unless otherwise indicated, all Scripture is taken from the New King James Version®. Copyright © 1982 by Thomas Nelson. Used by permission. All rights reserved.

Scripture quotations marked ESV are taken from the ESV® Bible (The Holy Bible, English Standard Version®) copyright © 2001 by Crossway, a publishing ministry of Good News Publishers. Used by permission. All rights reserved. Scripture quotations marked NASB are taken from the New American Standard Bible®, Copyright © 1960, 1962, 1963, 1968, 1971, 1972, 1973, 1975, 1977, 1995, 2020 by The Lockman Foundation. Used by permission. www.Lockman.org Scripture quotations marked NIV are taken from The Holy Bible, New International Version® NIV® Copyright © 1973, 1978, 1984, 2011 by Biblica, Inc.™ Used by permission. All rights reserved worldwide. Scripture quotations marked (NLT) are taken from the Holy Bible, New Living Translation, copyright © 1996, 2004, 2015 by Tyndale House Foundation. Used by permission of Tyndale House Publishers, a Division of Tyndale House Ministries, Carol Stream, Illinois 60188. All rights reserved.

Design and typesetting | garborgdesign.com

Printed in China

21 22 23 24 25 5 4 3 2 1

Contents

Introduction

Inside of every born again believer is an insatiable hunger to draw close and then closer to God. There is only one way to accomplish this heavenly desire within us, and it is to read the Word of God, meditate on it, and then declare it at all times!

Discovering afresh His wonderful promises and then declaring them out loud can renew our faith. We've chosen a theme to declare each month—*the Word, faith, fruitfulness, the name of Jesus, blessing, love, freedom from fear, strength, healing, the Holy Spirit, praise,* and *salvation*!

What do you do when it's March where you're declaring the truths about fruitfulness and you need freedom from fear? Jump over to the Scriptures and declarations in July. See what happens as you meditate on and declare God's powerful Word. Read each day's Scripture several times during the day until the Word of God sticks to your ribs and gets into your heart! And declare it out loud so you can hear it: So then faith comes by hearing, and hearing by the Word of God (see Romans 10:17).

You may even want to get your Bible out and read several verses before and after the selection so that the whole meaning of the Scripture will come alive in your spirit! Or try reading all the declarations for that month every day!

It's an extra blessing to see family unity strengthened by declaring and reading God's Word together. Fussing, complaining, and arguing turns to praising and loving God and each other in Jesus' name! This is one of the most powerful things that has ever happened in our lives—let it happen in yours!

The time you dedicate to the Word of God will be the most valuable time you have ever spent! I believe your spirit will soar because the amazing love of God that will come forth with power and truth. Each Scripture was selected to inspire you into a higher plane of love for Jesus, and the declarations provide a way for you to go directly into the very presence of God.

Joan Hunter
joanhunter.org

JANUARY

The Word

In the beginning God created the heavens and the earth.
GENESIS 1:1

God took nothing and from nothing He created the universe. How did He create it? From Hebrews 11:3, we get the important clue which can unlock the entire Bible to you in a totally new and different way: By faith, we understand that the worlds were framed by the Word of God, so that the things which are seen were not made of things which are visible.

It is by the Word of God, not by the hands of God nor by the feet of God, mind of God, or power of God. The Word of God frames our faith. We can create a whole new world for ourselves by speaking the Word of God for our lives!

It's one thing to read the Word of God, but it's another thing to memorize the Word of God. Get the Word of God in you. Possess it and declare, "It's mine. It's mine. It's mine! I take it for myself!"

God's Word Gives Me Discernment

For the word of God is living and active, sharper than any two-edged sword, piercing to the division of soul and of spirit, of joints and of marrow, and discerning the thoughts and intentions of the heart.

HEBREWS 4:12, ESV

Father, nothing can withstand the sword of your Word, which is mightier and more forceful than all the nuclear power in this world. With that sword in my hand each and every day, there's nothing I can't overcome. I'm a winner, not a loser, because your Word has made it so. I delight and revel in the power of your wonderful Word, which cleanses my heart, lifts my thoughts heavenward and is like an invincible two-edged sword preparing the way. It's quick, too, because it doesn't take long to hit the target.

I Have the Mind of Christ

For "who has known the mind of the LORD that he may instruct Him?" But we have the mind of Christ.
1 CORINTHIANS 2:16

Father, what a privilege it is to know that I'm not operating with a natural mind. I praise you that my thoughts are heavenly because I have the mind of Christ! I thank you that I don't have to worry about the silly things that come into my mind every once in a while, because when they start, I can just relax and realize that I have the mind of Christ. I don't have to hang on to the garbage and worries of the world, but instead, I'm concentrating on my eternal destination. I thank you, Father, and praise you for that!

God's Word Never Fails

So shall My word be that goes forth from My mouth;
It shall not return to Me void,
But it shall accomplish what I please,
And it shall prosper in the thing for which I sent it.
ISAIAH 55:11

Father, I thank you that your Word does everything—all that you say it will do. I thank you that it accomplishes exactly what you say, without any ifs, ands or buts. I thank you for the knowledge that your Word never says anything that will fall by the wayside and die. I praise you because you've said it never returns to you void. Your Word grows, multiplies, thrives, flourishes, and blooms wherever and whenever you send it. I praise you that it never dies on the vine but is constantly growing and multiplying!

God's Word Is Hidden in My Heart

Jesus replied, "But even more blessed are all who hear the word of God and put it into practice."
LUKE 11:28

Father, I bless you because I am blessed! I have heard your Word, and I keep it hidden in my heart that I might not sin against you. I thank you that because I keep your Word, I am blessed in everything I do. I thank you that I have had the opportunity to hear your Word. Father, I am blessed among all the people of every nation in the world because I have the ability to hear your Word. I thank you for your Word, which permeates my entire being and blesses me as I read, memorize, and declare it! Father, I am keeping it in my heart forever, and I love you for giving your Word!

I Am Walking in Righteousness

*All Scripture is inspired by God
and profitable for teaching, for reproof,
for correction, for training in righteousness.*
2 TIMOTHY 3:16, NASB

Father, I praise you that there is no guesswork with Scripture. I thank you for the knowledge that you inspired every word, and you had many purposes in inspiring those men of old to write down your thoughts because it establishes truth and godly principles for us to live by. I praise you, Father, that your Word has power to rebuke, admonish, and censure us. When I get out of line, your Word is right there to correct me and help me straighten out again. Thank you for giving me instructions on how to live in the beauty of your righteousness! I'm walking in righteousness today!

God's Word Is Everlasting

Heaven and earth will pass away,
but My words will by no means pass away.
MARK 13:31

Father, how I praise you because your Word will
never pass away. Friends are transient. Possessions
are subject to change. But your Word cannot! Even
when everything else fades away or goes down
the drain, your words shall remain forever and
forever. Even though we come into this world in
a perishable container, which we know won't last
forever, you have given us something to put into
our temporary housing that will last eternally: your
Word! Thank you, Father. When the storms of life
are thundering around me and it looks as though
everything may fall apart, I stand on the secure
knowledge that your words shall never pass away!

God's Word Sustains Me

And Jesus answered him, "It is written,
'Man shall not live by bread alone.'"
LUKE 4:4, ESV

I praise you, Father, for the spiritual banquet
you've given me in your Word. I feast every day on
this manna, and my body thrives on the heavenly
vitamins you provide. I thank you that I do not
have to live by physical things alone, but I can find
spiritual health in your Word, which assures me
of a healthy body, a sound mind, and an endless
supply of enthusiasm for tackling the tasks you
put before me each day. Jesus, you are the Bread of
Life! Thank you for making each and every word in
Scripture count in my life. I love you for that!

God Abides in Me

If you abide in me, and my words abide in you,
ask whatever you wish, and it will be done for you.
JOHN 15:7, NIV

Father, I love the word *abide*. I praise you that as
long as I dwell, reside, live, submit, and let your
words settle deep inside of me, you have given me
the awesome privilege of asking whatever I will.
I rest safely and securely in the knowledge that
what I ask will be done for me. You simply gave
me those two little conditions—that I abide in you
and let your words abide in me—for those blessings
of Abraham to overtake and overcome me. So I do
that, Father. Come abide in me and I abide in you.
You are a generous God who promises me every
good thing.

God Honors His Word

"I am ready to perform My word."
JEREMIAH 1:12

Father, you lose no time performing your Word. I can see you in my mind speeding up and expediting all the things you've promised because you are not a God who sits back and does nothing, but you are a God of action! I thank you that you make short work of those things, which stand in the way of the performance of your Word. Father, you don't use delaying tactics like the devil, but you are prompt and right on schedule at all times in fulfilling your Word!

God's Word Stands Firm

*I have hidden your word in my heart
that I might not sin against you....
Your word, L*ORD*, is eternal;
it stands firm in the heavens.*
PSALM 119:11, 89, NIV

Father, thank you for letting me hide your wonderful, brilliant, shining, glorious words in my heart for the purpose of having them there to remind me not to sin. Your words are so sharp and penetrating; they can go through the greatest temptation that might ever come my way to protect me from the fiery darts of the devil himself. I praise you for that weapon with which to protect myself at all times from sin. And how I thank you, Father, that we have no arguing and debating about your Word because it has been settled in heaven for eternity! I live by your heaven-made rules and don't have to depend on the peculiarities of humans to live by! I love your Word.

God's Word Gives Me Direction

Your word is a lamp to my feet
and a light to my path.
PSALM 119:105, ESV

Father, I thank you that I'm not stumbling around in the dark wondering which way to go. You have put your Word unto my feet so that I may receive understanding and enlightenment to my mind, my heart, and my soul! Father, I love your law, and I meditate in it day and night because of the glorious light it sheds abroad. I thank you that the path on which I walk is one where I have no fear that I might fall down in the darkness. My path is flooded with light with no hiding places for sin to lurk and get me. Thank you that your light is brighter than any light of this world, and it's turned right onto my path!

God's Word Is Light

The teaching of your word gives light,
so even the simple can understand.
PSALM 119:130, NLT

Father, I thank you that your Word broke through the cold, stony heart I once had. I praise you that when one single word sneaked through that crevice in my sinful armor, it began to give light to my life. Thank you that the unfolding of your Word gave me understanding, discernment, and comprehension. I long for your words to give me more and more light. Be merciful to me, show me your favor, establish my steps, and direct them by means of your Word! I love your Word, so I'll keep on hearing, receiving, loving, and obeying!

God's Word Is Priceless

The law from your mouth is more precious to me
than thousands of pieces of silver and gold.
PSALM 119:72, NIV

Father, I bless you that the world can have its silver and gold with its fluctuating prices, but your Word stands above all of the treasures of this world and never changes. I praise you because your promise surpasses anything this world has to offer. Thank you that it is better than silver and gold, houses and lands, or any other kind of material possessions. I thank you that the entrance of your Word illumines my entire life and teaches me wise and right discernment, good judgment and knowledge, and the Earth is full of your loving kindness and mercy.

God's Word Gives Wisdom

Therefore everyone who hears these words of mine and puts them into practice is like a wise man who built his house on the rock. The rain came down, the streams rose, and the winds blew and beat against that house; yet it did not fall, because it had its foundation on the rock.

MATTHEW 7:24–25, NIV

Father, I praise you that my house is built upon a rock because I have heard your Word, and I am a doer of the Word and not just a hearer. Because of this, you have called me a wise and productive man, who is practical in his ways. I bless you, Father, for the promise of your Word, which says that when the rains fell and the floods overflowed, and even when the winds became hurricane force and beat upon my house, it didn't fall because it was founded on a rock. My house will continue to stand on that solid rock!

God's Word Is Life

It is the Spirit who gives life;
the flesh profits nothing.
The words that I speak to you are spirit,
and they are life.

JOHN 6:63

Father, I praise you that the Holy Spirit quickens your Word. I thank you that the Spirit is the Life-giver because there is no profit in the flesh. I thank you that the words you have spoken and recorded in your Word give me spirit and life. I bless you, Father, that I am not dead in the trespasses of sin and disaster, but I am alive because my spirit has been quickened, energized, and made alive by your words!

God Makes Me Greater

You are of God, little children,
and have overcome them,
because He who is in you is greater
than he who is in the world.

1 JOHN 4:4

Father, how I applaud and glorify your Word. I thank you for the magnificent promises in your Word. I thank you that your Son, Jesus Christ, lives in me, and He is greater and mightier than the devil and all his doings. I don't have to submit to his torment any longer because I know that I know that I know that what your Word tells me is true. You have said that there is a greater One living in me than is living in the world, and I believe, receive, declare, and possess this promise for myself! I thank you that regardless of how big the devil might look to me in certain situations, I can stand tall and look down on him, knowing that I have far more power than he does!

God's Word Gives Success

This Book of the Law shall not depart from your mouth, but you shall meditate in it day and night, that you may observe to do according to all that is written in it. For then you will make your way prosperous, and then you will have good success.

JOSHUA 1:8

Your Word is in my mouth, Father, and I'm not taking it out! For too many years, I had the filth of the devil coming out, and I like what you've given me. I praise you that I am made righteous and am in right standing with you because of your saving grace. I thank you that because I am walking according to your Word, I am prospering and am having good success. I praise you, Father, that I don't have to depend on the world for instructions on how to be successful. I can depend on your Word because you don't make provision for failure; you only make provision for success! I'm prospering! I'm successful! I'm blessed because you said so!

God's Word Leads Me

There is therefore now no condemnation to those who are in Christ Jesus, who do not walk according to the flesh, but according to the Spirit.

ROMANS 8:1

Father, I thank you that I walk in victory today and *every* day because the blood of the Lamb has redeemed me. I'm washed clean inside and out because the best detergent in the whole world is your precious blood. Therefore, I have no condemnation or guilt in my life because my sins are washed away *forever*! Father, I'm not interested in walking after the flesh, because that leads to death, but I'm walking after the law of the Spirit of life, which is the law of my new being, and it has freed me from the law of sin and death. Hallelujah! I'm not only walking, but I'm dancing in the newness of life!

My God Is for Me

What then shall we say to these things?
If God is for us, who can be against us.
ROMANS 8:31

Father, I praise and glorify you because *you are for me*! Together, you and I make a majority, and nothing and no one can stand against us. Father, by myself, I might not be so super, but with you, I'm a majority at all times. I thank you that I don't have to rely on my own strength, but I'm walking in your power and might. Together we can move mountains. Hallelujah! I'm victorious because you're on my side. The devil can't win against me. His demons can't win against me. You could make it without me, but I sure can't do it without you!

God's Word Renews Me

Therefore, if anyone is in Christ, he is a new creation.
The old has passed away; behold, the new has come.
2 CORINTHIANS 5:17, ESV

Father, I praise you that I am in Christ because I have been born again of the incorruptible seed that can't be contaminated, spoiled, or tainted! I thank you that I am a *new* creature. I praise you that the individual who was me no longer exists. I praise you that all of the things of my old nature have passed away, and I'm a brand new creature in Christ. I praise you that everything about me has changed and that all things are *new*! I praise you that the month of January always ushers in a new year, and it reminds me of the newness of life in Christ Jesus. I praise you for making me and keeping me *new*!

God Makes All Things New

Don't lie to each other, for you have stripped off your old sinful nature and all its wicked deeds. Put on your new nature, and be renewed as you learn to know your Creator and become like him.

COLOSSIANS 3:9–10, NLT

Glory to God, I'm a new creation! Father, I praise you for making the Christian life so simple, because you so beautifully tell us what to do and what not to do. I have put off the old with all my evil ways, and have put on the new. I like the new me better! I thank you that my mind is renewed and is no longer conformed to this world because I have been created in your beautiful image. I love you, Father, and praise you for loving me so much that you put all these beautiful promises in your Word!

I Am in Covenant with God

"Behold, the days are coming, declares the Lord, when I will establish a new covenant with the house of Israel and with the house of Judah." ... "For this is the covenant that I will make with the house of Israel after those days, declares the Lord: I will put my laws into their minds, and write them on their hearts, and I will be their God, and they shall be my people."

HEBREWS 8:8,10, ESV

Father, I praise you and thank you for the new covenant, which you have given to us. You have written and imprinted your laws upon my innermost thoughts and understanding, and you have forever engraved them in my heart. I praise you for the way you have inscribed all of these laws permanently upon my heart, so wherever I go, I can never get away from you. Hallelujah! I'm a person of your new covenant!

I Walk in God's Love for Others

And now I plead with you...not as though I wrote a new commandment to you, but that which we have had from the beginning: that we love one another.
2 JOHN 5

Father, how I praise you that you instruct us to live the love-life and walk the love-life. I'm going to walk and talk the love-life at all times and love the unlovely. I praise you for the power you give me to walk this love-walk and for the instructions you give me. Father, let this year become the most loving of my life. I praise you for giving me a special infilling of your precious love.

God Calls Me
an Overcomer

*He who has an ear, let him hear what the Spirit
says to the churches. To him who overcomes I will give
some of the hidden manna to eat. And I will give him
a white stone, and on the stone a new name written
which no one knows except him who receives it.*

REVELATION 2:17

Father, I praise you for my ears that hear the
Spirit. I thank you for letting me be an overcomer
in all things through Christ who strengthens
me. I praise you that some day soon I will eat of
the hidden manna and will have a brand new
name written in stone—a name that is just for
me. Father, I praise you for your goodness to me.
I love you because I don't have to look at things
that are temporal because they are subject to
change. I look at those things that are eternal and
lasting. Hallelujah! My ears are hearing, and I'm
overcoming.

God's Word Is True

And he who was seated on the throne said, "Behold, I am making all things new." Also he said, "Write this down, for these words are trustworthy and true." And he said to me, "It is done! I am the Alpha and the Omega, the beginning and the end. To the thirsty I will give from the spring of the water of life without payment. The one who conquers will have this heritage, and I will be his God and he will be my son.

REVELATION 21:5–7, ESV

Jesus, you are the beginning and the end! Your words are true and faithful! You make all things, including me, brand new! When I was thirsty, you freely gave to me the water of life. I thank you for the power of the Holy Spirit; I am an overcomer at all times, and because of this, I shall inherit all things. God, you are my God, and Jesus, your redemptive work at Calvary made me God's child. Hallelujah!

I Am Free from Sin

*Knowing this, that our old man was crucified
with Him, that the body of sin might be done away
with, that we should no longer be slaves of sin. For he
who has died has been freed from sin.*

ROMANS 6:6–7

Father, how I thank you that with this *new* year,
because of my *new* life, my *old* self is crucified and
lifeless. I don't have to walk under sin's power and
dominion any longer. I praise you that the old,
unregenerate, unrenewed self is dead, dead, dead!
Therefore, I don't have to serve sin any longer. Sin
is no longer my master. When I learned to die to
self, you freed me from sin, wickedness, impurity,
iniquity, and error. I am now a servant to a new
Master who has revitalized me in the newness of
Christ!

I Walk in the Spirit

Jesus answered, "Most assuredly, I say to you, unless one is born of water and the Spirit, he cannot enter the kingdom of God. That which is born of the flesh is flesh, and that which is born of the Spirit is spirit."

JOHN 3:5-6

Father, I praise you that I am living in newness of life because I have been born again by your priceless Spirit. I thank you that I am no longer a fleshly creature, subject to the things of this world, but because I have been born again, I am a spirit-being under your control. I praise you that you provided such a pleasant and simple way for me to have eternal life! I'm walking toward the kingdom of God with a lift in my walk because I'm a new creation!

I Am Transformed by God's Word

Do not conform to the pattern of this world,
but be transformed by the renewing of your mind.
Then you will be able to test and approve what God's
will is—his good, pleasing and perfect will.
ROMANS 12:2, NIV

Father, I thank you that in my new life I do not have to be conformed to this world. I don't have to dress the way they do. I don't have to act the way the world acts, and I don't have to talk the way the world does. My new life gives me freedom to live the way you want me to. I thank you that my mind is renewed with new ideas, ideals, and attitudes. Father, I present my body and all its members to you as a living sacrifice because it is my reasonable and intelligent service to you. I praise you and thank you for your grace, which made this all possible. I shall glory in you forever! How perfect are your ways! They are faultless, spotless, and unblemished!

God's Not Finished Yet

Being confident of this very thing,
that He who has begun a good work in you
will complete it until the day of Jesus Christ.
PHILIPPIANS 1:6

Father, I praise you for confidence in my new life. Even though I can't always see the end of what you have planned for me, I have the complete knowledge and faith that you will keep working in me until the day of Jesus Christ. I praise you, Father, because I don't have to worry. You have promised it in your Word! You're still working in me and because of this, I'm an overcomer confident that whatever is born of you overcomes the whole world. So I'm going to shout, "I'm an overcomer! I'm an overcomer because God is working in me!"

I Am Reconciled to Christ

But now he has reconciled you by Christ's physical body through death to present you holy in his sight, without blemish and free from accusation—if you continue in your faith, established and firm, and do not move from the hope held out in the gospel. This is the gospel that you heard and that has been proclaimed to every creature under heaven, and of which I, Paul, have become a servant.

COLOSSIANS 1:22–23, NIV

Father, how I praise you that I stand before you as a new creation because you have buried my sins in the deepest sea never to be remembered again! How I praise you for this. You said the only condition was that I fully believe the truth and stand in it firmly. Father, I do, I do, I do! You are the truth and I stand in the hope of the gospel. I'm standing tall and straight and can look the world straight in the eye because my sins are gone, gone, gone!

God Gives Me Total Victory

And we know that all things work together for good to those who love God, to those who are the called according to His purpose.

ROMANS 8:28

Everything, everything, *everything* that happens to me works together for my own good. I thank you that you can take the biggest mess and turn everything in it around so that it turns out for my good. Regardless of how dark and gloomy things look, I know it's working for my good. I praise you that when I call for help, the very tide of the battle turns and my enemies flee, all because of you! Thank you that you take any old mess and make a miracle out of it! Thank you, Father, for a month of total victory because I have stood on your promises. Thank you for the extra prosperity that has come into my house; thank you for the health you have given me; thank you for showing me that miracles and wonders still happen today. Thank you for the remarkable victory you have given me simply by declaring your promises and the truth of your Word.

FEBRUARY

Faith

The Christian life is so simple because we only have to do two things:

1. Do what God tells us to do.
2. Stop doing what He tells us not to do.

And how do we do what God wants us to do? The psalmist tells us: *"Your word I have hidden in my heart, that I might not sin against You"* (119:11).

Once you establish in your own mind that the Bible is the actual spoken Word of God written down for posterity, your faith can begin that upward climb as you read, declare, memorize, and hide the Word in your heart.

How do you increase your faith? *"Faith comes by hearing, and hearing by the word of God"* (Romans 10:17). We need to *hear* the Word of God.

How can we hear the Word of God? By reading the Bible. The Bible is God's personal love letter to you, and if you will just read it, believe it, declare it, and live it, then every promise in the Word is yours!

My Hope Increases My Faith

Now faith is the substance of things hoped for,
the evidence of things not seen.
HEBREWS 11:1

Thank you, Father, that faith is the pledge and the confirmation of the things I long and hope for, but which I can't see at the moment. Even though I don't see some things with my natural eyes, in my spirit I can see them as a reality. Because of this, I can see what is not revealed to my senses. Father, I thank you for Noah, who had never heard of rain, but because he was prompted by faith, he diligently constructed and prepared an ark through the eyes of faith. In the same way I can also look with my eyes of faith and see things come to pass which were just a hope in the past! Hallelujah!

By Faith I Will Seek God

But without faith it is impossible to please Him, for he who comes to God must believe that He is, and that He is a rewarder of those who diligently seek Him.

HEBREWS 11:6

Father, thank you for making it so plain that if I don't use the faith you've given me, there is no way I can please you. I don't have to work up something on my own because your faith is a gift. I believe in you and I believe that you are the God of all gods! I believe that you are a rewarder of those who diligently seek you. I will continue to diligently seek you, and I thank you for rewarding my faith. You've made your promises so easy for me to accept through faith! I am receiving those rewards right now!

I Will Carry My Shield of Faith

In all circumstances take up the shield of faith, with which you can extinguish all the flaming darts of the evil one.
EPHESIANS 6:16, ESV

Thank you, Father, for surrounding me with your shield of faith so that I am completely protected from every kind of wickedness. Any kind of wicked temptation, insult, accusation, or attack is quenched and conquered by the shield of faith that I wear constantly, and not even the devil himself can get through it! I walk in the world and I am not afraid. Nothing can harm me. I walk in faith! I talk in faith! I pray in faith, and I rejoice in faith! Father, you are my strength and my fortress, and I praise you because with my shield of faith, I live in victory every minute of the day, every day of the year!

My Faith Grows Daily

For by the grace given me I say to every one of you:
Do not think of yourself more highly than you ought,
but rather think of yourself with sober judgment, in
accordance with the faith God has distributed to each
of you.
ROMANS 12:3, NIV

Father, I thank you that you have given to me
the measure of faith I need to be exactly the kind
of person you want me to be, and to do all the
things you want me to do! We are all different and
distinct individuals, and yet you have given to each
of us the same measure of faith as everyone else,
so that I can take on the unique tasks that fit in
your perfect plan for me. I thank you that you have
given me just as much faith as anyone else in the
world because all your children are precious to you.
I'm using and developing my measure of faith daily!

My Faith Produces Results

*I pray that the sharing of your faith may become
effective for the full knowledge of every good thing that
is in us for the sake of Christ.*

PHILEMON 6

My faith produces good fruit in me! It produces
and promotes full recognition, appreciation,
understanding, and precise knowledge. I identify
myself with the ever-truthful God who cannot
deceive, and my faith grows, multiplies, and
abounds! I praise you for a sound mind; for the
salvation of my family; for health, wealth, and
happiness; for joy, love, peace, prosperity, and
abundance. I praise you for every good thing!
Hallelujah!

In God,
Everything Is Possible

*I can do all things through Christ
who strengthens me.*
PHILIPPIANS 4:13

Thank you for the faith to know that I am empowered through Jesus Christ to do *all things*! I can handle any situation because Jesus strengthens and equips me to succeed in even the most difficult situations and problems that I face. Through Christ, every obstacle has become a stepping-stone for me, every problem an opportunity. Through Christ, I have the willpower to overcome any and all of my bad habits. I thank you because your Word doesn't say I can only do some things through Christ which strengthens me, but it says *I can do all things*! Hallelujah, that's power! I thank you that I can live in divine health! I thank you because I can live in prosperity. I thank you that I can live in total victory!

I Will Live by Faith

Now the just shall live by faith;
but if anyone draws back,
My soul has no pleasure in him.
HEBREWS 10:38

Glory to God, I'm living by faith! I live by the confident conviction that you are God and I am your beloved child. I believe in you, cling to you, and trust in you, and because of this, I can rely wholly and continually on you through Jesus Christ! I bless you for the warning that if I draw back, you will have no pleasure in me. Father, I'm living in faith, walking in faith, talking in faith, and running in faith because I want to please you!

I Am Saved through Faith

For by grace you have been saved through faith,
and that not of yourselves; it is the gift of God.
EPHESIANS 2:8

I don't have to save myself! Hallelujah! I thank
you, Father, that I didn't do a thing to deserve
your unmerited favor, but because of your grace,
I have been delivered from judgment and made a
partaker of Christ's salvation. I thank you that it
was a beautiful gift that you just gave to me, not
something that I accomplished by my works or
striving. Salvation is mine because you loved me
so much that you sent your Son to save me from
perishing in the darkness of sin and death. I thank
you for the gift of everlasting life I have in Christ.
Because you have shown me the fullness of your
love, I love you, Father! I love your Son, Jesus Christ!
I love the new life you have given me through your
beloved Son!

I Am Delivered from Darkness

Giving thanks to the Father who has qualified us to be partakers of the inheritance of the saints in the light. He has delivered us from the power of darkness and conveyed us into the kingdom of the Son of His love.
COLOSSIANS 1:12–13

I will thank you and praise you forever, Father, because I am delivered! I've been taken out of the control and the dominion of darkness, changed so that I am qualified to share the inheritance of the saints, and translated into the kingdom of light! Glorious Father, how I praise you that because of your loving kindness and mercy, I have been made a partaker of the inheritance of all the saints! I've been delivered from bad habits, evil thoughts, and delivered from the very power of the devil! I want to say *thank you, thank you, thank you* because you have reached inside of me and turned me into a brand new person, and you have sent me straight into the kingdom of your beloved Son, Jesus Christ!

I Will Rejoice Today and Every Day

Rejoice in the Lord always.
Again I will say, rejoice!
PHILIPPIANS 4:4

I have so many wonderful reasons to rejoice in you, Father. I rejoice in your presence in my life! I rejoice in each new day you give me to live, to love, to enjoy, and to help others! I rejoice that I am your child and that you love me more than I love myself. I rejoice in your Word, in your power, and in your glory! I rejoice in the blessings you shower upon me day after day—blessings of joy, of health, of prosperity, of family, and of friends! I rejoice in the work you give me to do and in the quiet times in my day when I come to you and worship you. I rejoice when I'm tired, and I rejoice in you even when I am attacked by the devil. I delight in you even when my body is not feeling as I'd like. I rejoice at night. I rejoice during the day! God, you are really amazing!

I Rejoice in Righteousness

This righteousness is given through faith in Jesus Christ to all who believe. There is no difference between Jew and Gentile.

ROMANS 3:22, NIV

Glory to God! I have the righteousness of God in me because I have faith and personal trust in Jesus Christ! I praise you, Father, that your righteousness is available to everyone who believes in and confidently relies on Jesus, because that means I'm conformed to your Word and your promise! I'm rejoicing right now that I am marching in accordance with your plan! Thank you for filling me with your righteousness, because I'm using that loving righteousness with my family, my friends, and the people I work with every day. Father, I love your righteousness!

Nothing Can Separate Me from the Love of God

For I am convinced that neither death nor life, neither angels nor demons, neither the present nor the future, nor any powers, neither height nor depth, nor anything else in all creation, will be able to separate us from the love of God that is in Christ Jesus our Lord.

ROMANS 8:38–39, NIV

Father, my faith is rising to new heights! I thank you that I am in your love and that nothing, absolutely nothing, can separate me from your love! I'm overwhelmed that your Word has made it so clear—so powerfully plain and positive—that I can never be moved from your love, which is in Christ Jesus our Lord. I rejoice that your power guarantees me your eternal love, no matter what the devil or any of his demons try to pull, any time or any place. I'm living in your divine love, regardless of any and all circumstances!

Jesus Christ Lives in Me

I have been crucified with Christ; it is no longer I who live, but Christ lives in me; and the life which I now live in the flesh I live by faith in the Son of God, who loved me and gave Himself for me.
GALATIANS 2:20

Glory to God! I'm dead and alive at the same time! Thank you, precious Father, that I'm living a life that is really Jesus Christ living in me! I praise you, Father, because my worldly ways and sins were crucified on the cross with Jesus, who loved me and gave himself for me. The old me is dead—doubts, thoughts, habits, hurts, and memories—and I'm a completely new person, top to bottom, inside and out. Jesus rules the body I live in now, and I live in this body of flesh and bone by my faith in Him. Because of this, I'm a new person with nothing to hold me back! Father, I thank you that my new life glorifies you!

God's Love Surrounds Me Daily

For God so loved the world that He gave
His only begotten Son, that whoever believes in Him
should not perish but have everlasting life.
JOHN 3:16

Father, this is the day the world says is the day for lovers, but I don't have to depend on just this one day a year, because I'm living in your love every day of the year. Thank you that your love encompasses the entire world, and yet is personal just for me. Father, you said if I would simply believe in you, I would not perish, but have everlasting life. I believe, I believe, I believe! Thank you for the faith that lets me believe! I receive your gift of eternal life and I look forward to living forever with you.

I Speak Words of Faith

*If anyone speaks, let him speak as the oracles of God.
If anyone ministers, let him do it as with the ability
which God supplies, that in all things God may be
glorified through Jesus Christ, to whom belong the glory
and the dominion forever and ever. Amen.*

1 PETER 4:11

Father, I thank you that as I speak, I speak as a
prophet of God, because my mouth shall speak
your words. My words are like a honeycomb, sweet
to the soul and health to the bones. I praise you
because I have a wholesome tongue, which is a tree
of life. My mouth is also a well of life. I guard my
tongue so that I am not snared with the words of
my mouth. My soul retains your words, and out of
the abundance of my soul, shall I speak! Amen!

God Cares for Me

*Casting all your anxieties on him,
because he cares for you.*
1 PETER 5:7

Here are my cares, Father! This means *all* of my worries, anxieties, and concerns. I'm giving them all to you once and for all! Your love overwhelms me! I thank you for taking all of my worries and cares away because you love me so much and you don't want me to be burdened. My anxieties are gone! Just as in the story of the prodigal son, you don't care what I've done or where I've been; you love me and care for me no matter what. Father, I'm so glad to be home at last with you. I rejoice because I'm your child, forgiven and restored by your mercy and loving kindness to my inheritance in your kingdom. I praise you, Father, that my ways have been changed because you care for me! Hallelujah! I don't have any more worries I have cast them upon you.

God Healed My Heart

I will give you a new heart and put a new spirit within you; I will take the heart of stone out of your flesh and give you a heart of flesh.

EZEKIEL 36:26

Father, I'm so thankful that I have a new heart and a new spirit within me! Thank you, Father, that you've taken my stony heart out and replaced it with a heart filled to the brim with love! I love you! I love my friends! I love my family! I even love my enemies because of what you have done for me! I never have to worry about running out of love because you keep filling me up with more, more, more! I thank you, Father, that I can love you with all of this new heart you've given me, and I thank you that with my new spirit I now live righteously.

I Will Follow God's Light and Love

Then Jesus spoke to them again, saying,
"I am the light of the world.
He who follows Me shall not walk in darkness,
but have the light of life."

JOHN 8:12

It's fun walking in the light, Father, because Jesus is the light of the world! Thank you, Father, for the light you gave me through your Son, Jesus. By this wonderful, brilliant light I walked out of the gloom of darkness and left it behind forever! Now I can see the way because the path of new life in Jesus shines brightly. Darkness holds no more fear for me because it's gone from my life, and I am walking and leaping and praising God in the light! I glory in the light of Jesus, and I follow where He leads me. In His light, I am happy, I am healthy, and I am prosperous! In His light, I am fulfilled and victorious! His light *is* my life!

God Gives Me Wisdom

If any of you lacks wisdom, let him ask God,
who gives generously to all without reproach,
and it will be given him.
JAMES 1:5, ESV

I praise you, Father, because I have wisdom! I have
all the wisdom I need to prevail over any challenge.
Your Word says if I don't have it, all I have to do
is ask, and you will give it to me, liberally and
ungrudgingly. Thank you for giving me the kind
of wisdom that triumphs over worldly knowledge
every time, because worldly knowledge doesn't
compare to your wisdom. You are a giving God, so
I have all the wisdom I need to live and work and
make decisions righteously and victoriously. I have
wisdom in all my dealings with others, and I praise
and thank you for it!

God Is My Helper and Provider

Don't love money; be satisfied with what you have.
For God has said, "I will never fail you.
I will never abandon you."
So we can say with confidence,
"The Lord is my helper, so I will have no fear.
What can mere people do to me?"

HEBREWS 13:5–6, NLT

I am gloriously satisfied, Father, in the overflowing abundance of divine blessings you have showered upon my life! I am content in your love! I praise you that there isn't any room left in me for greed or for envy of what my neighbors have, because your constant presence in my life is wealth far above the material things of this world. I'm not afraid of what anybody can do to me since you've assured me that you are my helper, and no one can prevail over my all-powerful God. Father, I don't have to rely on worldly security, because you are everything I need! I praise you because you never relax your hold on me. You never let me go! Glory!

I Speak by Faith and Authority

For assuredly, I say to you, whoever says to this mountain, "Be removed and be cast into the sea," and does not doubt in his heart, but believes that those things he says will be done, he will have whatever he says.

MARK 11:23

Jesus, I believe in you and your holy Word! Your Word and your promises empower me to have what I desire when I pray. My desires align with your Word and what you want for me. Therefore, I say I have wisdom! I have health! I have happiness! I have prosperity! I have abundance! I have joy! I have love! Father, I say to every mountain in my life, "Be removed and be cast into the sea." Jesus, you give me strength and perseverance to face every obstacle that arises. No mountain will stand in the way of following you and your will for my life.

I Pray by Faith

Therefore I say to you,
whatever things you ask when you pray,
believe that you receive them,
and you will have them.

MARK 11:24

Father, I believe right now! I've prayed, and the minute the words came out of my mouth, I believed! I thank you, Father, that you didn't tell me to wait until I built up enough faith to believe, but to believe the very instant I prayed so that I could have the things that I desired. I praise you, Father, that because I take delight in you, you give me the desires of my heart, and that's why I know, that I know, that I *know* that you're going to fulfill the desires that you yourself have placed there! Glory, Father! Thank you for the faith you've given to me to see this come to pass.

God Satisfies My Thirst

On the last and greatest day of the festival, Jesus stood and said in a loud voice, "Let anyone who is thirsty come to me and drink. Whoever believes in me, as Scripture has said, rivers of living water will flow from within them."

JOHN 7:37–38, NIV

Father, I'm thirsty, thirsty, thirsty! I'm drinking at your streams of living water deeper and deeper all the time. I thank you because that same river of living water I'm drinking now blesses me and blesses everyone around me as it flows from my innermost being. Father, I praise you for giving to me a river of living water that never runs dry, but keeps flowing and flowing. Thank you for that refilling station you've given me to use day and night. Thank you because it is open twenty-four hours a day. Father, I love you for that!

I Am Redeemed and Set Free

Be sure of this:
The wicked will not go unpunished,
but those who are righteous will go free.
PROVERBS 11:21, NIV

Father, how I praise you for such a promise. My faith is in you and not in what I see. I see much wickedness around me, but you are holy, just, and true. You see the works of the wicked and you will make all things right in due time. The wicked will be overthrown and the house of the righteous will stand. *My* house will stand because we are standing on the promises of your Word. You have set me free and I will enjoy eternal life because of your saving grace. Thank you!

I Am Fruitful and Pleasing to God

For this reason we also, since the day we heard it, do not cease to pray for you, and to ask that you may be filled with the knowledge of His will in all wisdom and spiritual understanding; that you may walk worthy of the Lord, fully pleasing Him, being fruitful in every good work and increasing in the knowledge of God.

COLOSSIANS 1:9–10

Father, I praise you that I am being filled with the knowledge of your will in all wisdom and spiritual understanding. I thank you that I am constantly learning your ways and purposes and that you are giving me discernment of spiritual things. I praise you because you have given me these blessings, I am walking worthy of you, Lord, and am fruitful in every good work, steadily growing and increasing in my knowledge of you. I thank you that all my decisions are ordered by you! Glory!

The Joy of the Lord Is My Strength

*I am coming to you now, but I say these things while
I am still in the world, so that they may have the full
measure of my joy within them.*
JOHN 17:13, NIV

Father, I thank you because I am filled with joy!
The joy of the Lord is my strength, so I'm strong
because my cup is filled to the top and overflowing
with joy. You have anointed me with the oil of
gladness. I sing and shout with joy because I have
favor with God and man, so I'm always a winner.
My joy is contagious and flows over to reach others,
and today I'm speaking love, joy, and peace to
everyone I meet. Thank you for telling me the
things that have put joy in my heart! I'm running,
running, running because your full measure of joy
is within me.

God Made Me a New Creation

For you have been born again not of seed
which is perishable but imperishable, that is,
through the living and enduring word of God.
1 PETER 1:23, NASB

I'm born again of incorruptible seed! Father, I can't thank and praise you enough for lifting me out of the darkness and sin of the world, where mortal life leads only to death. Your Word makes me made new, regenerated, and reborn to eternal life in your kingdom. I am in this world of corruption and decay, but I am not of it because the perfect seed of your Word has made me into an entirely new person. Father, I praise you that your Word lives and abides forever! Because of this, I shall live forever, too!

I Am a Child of God

*The Spirit Himself bears witness with our spirit that we
are children of God, and if children, then heirs—heirs
of God and joint heirs with Christ, if indeed we suffer
with Him, that we may also be glorified together.*
ROMANS 8:16–17

Father, how I thank you for letting me clearly
know that I can never be lost or alone because the
Holy Spirit says that I am your child! I know where
I belong. Thank you, Father, that I am a joint heir
with Jesus. You gave everything you had to Him so
I share fully in the entire inheritance. Father, I'm
so rich because of your promises. Because I am a
joint heir with Jesus, I am your temple and your
Spirit dwells in me! I thank you that I have power
to overcome all obstacles in this world. You are my
God and I am your child. I claim your promise that
all things in heaven and earth belong to me!

I Choose Faith over Fear

Therefore I say to you, do not worry about your life, what you will eat or what you will drink; nor about your body, what you will put on. Is not life more than food and the body more than clothing?

MATTHEW 6:25

Thank you, Father, for another beautiful month where I had the opportunity to love you more than ever before and to study and grow in your Word. Father, your Word and your promises have become real in my life in ways that make me love you more and more. I thank you that your Word endures forever and that I have victory in you. I don't have to take thought for my life because my life is in you, Father, and you supply *everything*. I thank you that the kingdom of God is not meat and drink, but righteousness, peace, and joy in the Holy Ghost. I have health! I have abundance! I have joy! I have peace! I have Jesus!

MARCH

Abundance

Jesus came that we would have abundant life (see John 10:10). He wants us to be fruitful and bear *much* fruit—spiritually, physically, emotionally, and mentally...at home, work, in our relationships, finances, health, and more.

And He told us how we can be fruitful: *"Abide in Me, and I in you. As the branch cannot bear fruit of itself, unless it abides in the vine, neither can you, unless you abide in Me. I am the vine, you are the branches. He who abides in Me, and I in him, bears much fruit; for without Me you can do nothing"* (John 15:4–5).

As you meditate on the following Scriptures and declarations this month, let them draw you into His presence to be near to His heart and abide with him. Glorify Jesus by bearing much fruit and living in His abundance, because Jesus said, *"By this My Father is glorified, that you bear much fruit; so you will be My disciples"* (John 15:8).

My Soul Prospers

*Beloved, I pray that you may prosper in all things
and be in health, just as your soul prospers.*
3 JOHN 2

Father, I rejoice in the desire you have for
prosperity and health in my body and my soul!
Thank you for being such a wonderful and loving
Father who takes care of me in such full and
overflowing measure. Thank you for the secret
of prosperity, which lies in giving to you so that
you can multiply it back to me. I'm not going to
hold tight to what I have, Father, but instead, I'm
keeping my hands empty and open so you can
keep filling them up with more! And I'm placing
the same trust in you for my health, knowing
how generously you provide. Thank you for the
blessing of wonderful and divine health that I live
in all this year. Your Word is my life, so my soul is
prospering!

Heaven's Floodgates Are Open in My Life

"Bring the whole tithe into the storehouse,
that there may be food in my house. Test me in this,"
says the LORD Almighty, "and see if I will not throw
open the floodgates of heaven and pour out so much
blessing that there will not be room enough
to store it."

MALACHI 3:10, NIV

Here it is, Father, my whole tithe. I'm giving it to you! You are the best financial advisor I could possibly have! I'm giving generously into your storehouse, Almighty God, because it pleases you to "throw open the floodgates of heaven" and to let the blessings gush out in abundance upon me. I am made in your image, so I know you want me to be generous as you are generous in giving to me until I have no room for more! I receive the gift of your blessed abundance with thanks and praise, and I'm giving to you, Father, fully trusting in your promise of return. I'm expanding my mind and my ability to receive your blessings to make more room for that flood that is pouring out of those floodgates.

I Receive God's Favor

To the person who pleases him, God gives wisdom,
knowledge and happiness, but to the sinner he gives the
task of gathering and storing up wealth to hand it over
to the one who pleases God.
ECCLESIASTES 2:26, NIV

Father, those who do not follow you are
working to gather and store up wealth to give
to the righteous who are in right standing with
you. Glory! Thank you for giving me wisdom,
knowledge, and happiness! I rejoice because
you teach me that covetousness and greed are
meaningless, for you take the wealth sinners have
gained and give it to those who please you, for your
way is righteousness. I receive that sinner's money
right now so I can have more to give to you. I'm
blessed by your marvelous generosity, Father.

I Receive a Multiplied Harvest

Cast your bread upon the waters,
for you will find it after many days.
ECCLESIASTES 11:1

Heavenly Father, I love to cast my bread upon your waters, and I praise you for the way you multiply it and send back many times over what I give! Thanks for showing me that the real secret of receiving is to give with a loving heart, because when I put my whole trust in you, everything always comes back magnified. Father, I thank you that I am able to give love, kindness, a helping hand, time, money, and gifts whenever you tell me because it's your good pleasure to replace it to me from your own unlimited store house. I've cast my bread upon the water, Father, and I thank you for the great harvest that is coming back to me!

I Will Seek God First

*But seek first the kingdom of God
and His righteousness,
and all these things shall be added to you.*
MATTHEW 6:33

Father, I praise and thank you for the truth of
the promises in your Word! You said *all things*
shall be added to me, and I believe every word of
it! I am craving and earnestly seeking everything
in the kingdom of God. You never fail me. You
have gathered me into your kingdom and your
righteousness, and here I am, jubilantly rejoicing
because of it! You give me everything I need, not
because of what I do or don't do, but because I'm a
member of your very own family, loved and cared for,
from now through eternity. I hold out my hands to
you, Father, and claim your promise that *all* things
are added to me. I have love, joy, peace of mind,
health, and abundance. I have *all* things! Father,
you're so good to me that I can't glorify you enough!

God Is My Sun and Shield

For the LORD God is a sun and shield;
the LORD bestows favor and honor;
no good thing does he withhold
from those whose walk is blameless.

PSALM 84:11, NIV

Father, you are my sun and shield! I love you for promising that you will not withhold one single good thing from me. I rejoice to walk uprightly in your light because in your light, I can always know how to handle any situation. Your shield protects me from the devil's barbs, his lies, his deceits, and I rejoice that he runs away from your light! Protected by your shield and illumined by your light, my life is blessed by an abundance of your gifts, for you are a God of grace and glory! I glorify your name, Father, because you supply all my needs and more! Thank you for the heavenly bliss and favor you generously bestow on me. I confidently commit all I am and all I have to you!

I Give and Receive Abundantly

Give, and you will receive. Your gift will return to you in full—pressed down, shaken together to make room for more, running over, and poured into your lap. The amount you give will determine the amount you get back.
LUKE 6:38, NLT

Father, how I bless you for your money-back guarantee, which guarantees that when I give to you, it shall be given back to me. When I give love, you give me an exceeding abundance of love. When I give time, you return that time to me over and over again. When I give money, you give it back to me in full and plenteous amounts. I praise you that you use what I give as a measuring spoon to dish out what you give to me, so I don't ever need to be limited by anything except what I am willing to give. Father, I'm giving my all and everything I am and have to you, and I thank you that I am walking in a super abundant supply!

I Will Give Generously

Remember this:
Whoever sows sparingly will also reap sparingly,
and whoever sows generously will also reap generously.
2 CORINTHIANS 9:6

How I praise you, Father, for the wonderful harvest you are bringing forth in my garden! Thank you for teaching me how to be a successful farmer. Thank you for teaching me to sow generously and joyfully in great abundance so you can bless it and return it to me multiplied beyond my wildest dreams! Thank you for the harvest you have prepared for me. Thank you for teaching me not to be stingy in any area of my life, whether it is in love, health, joy, or finances. I plant in faith, generously, and you open the floodgates of heaven to pour blessings on me! I thank and praise you, Father, for the exploding abundance of all things you bring about from the seeds of my giving!

I Will Store My Treasure in Heaven

Do not lay up for yourselves treasures on earth, where moth and rust destroy and where thieves break in and steal; but lay up for yourselves treasures in heaven, where neither moth nor rust destroys and where thieves do not break in and steal. For where your treasure is, there your heart will be also.

MATTHEW 6:19–21

I'm not storing my treasures up here on the earth, but I'm storing them up in heaven with you, Father, where I don't have to worry about moths and rust, or even thieves who break through and steal. Father, I'm banking my treasure with you because you are the most reliable trust company in the entire world. You are a living river of blessings, and I praise you for taking care of your children with loving interest! My treasure is in heaven with you, and my heart is right up there too!

God Will Supply My Needs

And my God shall supply all your need according to His riches in glory by Christ Jesus.
PHILIPPIANS 4:19

My needs are gloriously and liberally supplied! Thank you, Father, for sending Jesus to die on the cross as a ransom for my sins because through Him I have abundant new life! I praise you not only for paying all my bills, but also for taking care of me in countless invisible ways: providing love when I need it, lifting my spirit, sending a friend when I need a helping hand, directing your angels to guard my family. Over and over, you surprise me with your miraculous timing in providing answers to even unspoken prayers of mine! Father, I rejoice that my needs are fulfilled—faithfully and constantly—by your wonderful and inexhaustible riches found in glory by Christ Jesus!

My Cup Runs Over

The bin of flour was not used up,
nor did the jar of oil run dry,
according to the word of the LORD
which He spoke by Elijah.

1 KINGS 17:16

My jar of oil shall never fail, because I shall never eat my seed! I praise you, Father, that when the widow was willing to listen to your prophet and share what she had instead of eating it all with her son, you kept filling the barrel of meal and pouring oil into the jar. Father, how we bless you for giving us instructions on how to have our needs met at all times. I praise you that even though the supply looks low at times, I can rest assured that you're always there to put in what I need!

I Will Seek God Daily

I love those who love me; and those who diligently seek me will find me. Riches and honor are with me, enduring wealth and righteousness. My fruit is better than gold, even pure gold, and my yield better than choicest silver. I walk in the way of righteousness, in the midst of the paths of justice, to endow those who love me with wealth, that I may fill their treasuries.

PROVERBS 8:17–21, NASB

Father, how I love your Word and all the promises you have for me. I thank you that enduring wealth and uprightness in every area of my life is mine! I thank you that you even allow me to inherit substance, often from sources I never knew about, and that you fill my treasuries. I am indeed wealthy because my riches are heavenly and divine. Thank you that you have taken charge of my earthly bank account and fill it with divine deposits! Glory!

My Home Is Blessed

*The curse of the LORD is on the house of the wicked,
but He blesses the habitation of the just.*
PROVERBS 3:33

Father, my house is blessed! I rejoice that you are
a God of justice. No thought or act escapes your
notice, and you know which are the houses of the
wicked and which are the houses of the righteous.
You see through all the deceptions of the wicked;
there is no way they can hide from your curse. But
I praise you because you also see directly into the
hearts and minds of the righteous, and you never
forget to bless and reward your children who serve
you faithfully. Look into my heart and my mind,
dear Father, because I rejoice in praising you! I
glory in your wonderful blessings!

I Receive God's Endless Love

The blessing of the LORD makes one rich,
and He adds no sorrow with it.
PROVERBS 10:22

I praise you, Father, for filling my life with the treasure of your blessing, which makes me rejoice day after day. I am rich in you! I am rich in your endless love, which feeds me like manna from heaven! You put food on my table, clothes on my back, and smiles on my face and the faces of my family! Glory, Father! How can I thank you enough? You give me health, happiness, and prosperity! You guard me from temptation and teach me with the wisdom of your Word! You renew and refresh my spirit so I can face each day with joy! Father, I praise you for not adding sorrow to my life, because with all your blessings, there just isn't room for it!

I Ask, Seek, Knock, and Receive

And so I tell you, keep on asking, and you will receive what you ask for. Keep on seeking, and you will find. Keep on knocking, and the door will be opened to you. For everyone who asks, receives. Everyone who seeks, finds. And to everyone who knocks, the door will be opened.

LUKE 11:9-10, NLT

Glory! Hallelujah! Hallelujah, Father! I'm an asker, a seeker, and a knocker, and because of this, I'm a receiver. Thank you that your Word says if I ask it shall be given to me! Thank you that you didn't say *some* will receive but you said *everyone*, including me! When I ask, *you* give to me; when I knock, *you* open the door; when I seek, *you* guide me safely to my destination. I'm asking, Father, and therefore, I have what I ask for. I have love! I have joy! I have health! I have prosperity! Thank you for being such a loving and generous Father to me!

God Is My Provider

He provides food for those who fear him;
he remembers his covenant forever.
PSALM 111:5, ESV

Oh, glorious Father, you are the river of life, the provider of all my well-being! I rejoice every day because you remember me without fail. You not only put the food on my table, but you nourish my soul and protect me from all physical harm. Because I am your child, you love me. I eat the food you give me with a hearty appetite, delighting in each bite because I know who has provided it and who will always provide it. Father, I am thankful for everything you give me, for it all belongs to you. I am blessed by your caring, sharing, loving, and wonderful faithful-ness to me! Hallelujah! I praise you that your covenant is forever imprinted on your mind so that you will remember it throughout all of eternity.

God Is My Shepherd

The LORD is my shepherd;
I shall not want.

PSALM 23:1

You are my shepherd and I shall not want. I shall not want for health! I shall not want for finances! Father, your promises are magnificent, *big* promises! Your love for me is so great that you want me to have every good thing! I thank you and praise you, heavenly Father, because you say plainly and clearly that I shall not want! You are my God, and I am your child! You are my shepherd, and I follow where you lead! I rejoice because you are the kind of Father who wants me to personally prosper in this life and share your eternal glory in the next! Father, I'm blessed beyond words! I shall not want for joy! I shall not want for happiness!

God Is My Salvation

Blessed be the Lord,
Who daily loads us with benefits,
The God of our salvation!

PSALM 68:19

I'm loaded, but not with problems! Father, I thank you for loading me with the good things of life every day! I don't have to live on yesterday's blessings or wait for tomorrow's blessings because you send fresh blessings each day. I'm singing and shouting my praises up to you because you give me a taste of heaven right on this earth! You are the God of my salvation and all glory belongs to you. Every moment of this day is special to me because you are always right here with me, and you know what benefits I need much better than I do! I love you, praise you, and bless your name, Father, for all I'm receiving today. Thank you that I don't have to have only monthly or weekly blessings, but that you supply them on a daily basis! Hallelujah!

God Gives Good Gifts

Yes, the LORD will give what is good,
and our land will yield its increase.
PSALM 85:12, ESV

I can't help praising you, Father, because you know how to give good gifts. You have given me life and you have removed the curse of sin from my life through the sacrifice of your only begotten Son on the cross. I thank you for my new life and my salvation. I thank you for Jesus Christ. I thank you for the Holy Spirit. Yes, Father, you give what is good and my heart rejoices. My arms are open wide to receive your gifts! I love you with all my heart, all my soul, all my mind, and all my strength. Because of your goodness, Father, my land is blessed with a rich harvest and I am prosperous.

I Walk in Obedience and Blessing

*And all these blessings shall come upon you
and overtake you, because you obey the voice
of the LORD your God.*

DEUTERONOMY 28:2

I'm ready, Father, to be overcome and overtaken with blessings! I will not listen to the devil; I'm listening to your voice only. I've cleaned out my ears, and I'm hearing even the tiniest little word you say to me. I'm singing your praises and rejoicing because you've promised that your blessing will catch up with me and simply overwhelm me. I want to watch them arrive, Father, because I've inherited even the blessings you gave to Abraham. Because Jesus took my sins away, I am restored to your favor. I praise you for the abiding love you have for your people, which has flowed down through the centuries to reach me. I bless you because I live under your blessings. I heard the condition to your blessings too, Father, so I'm doing my part and following your instructions completely!

God's Blessing Remains on My Life

*Blessed shall you be in the city,
and blessed shall you be in the country.*

DEUTERONOMY 28:3

Heavenly Father, you will bless me wherever I am—in the city or the country. I rejoice that your blessing follows me wherever I go! I thank you that you are my shield and protection from evil in the city! I thank you that you are my strength and my rest in the field! You are with me wherever I go, so that my way is blessed and prosperous. My work goes well and my life bears fruit that pleases you. Because you love and bless me, I am not swallowed up in the confusion and darkness of the world. I rejoice, Father, because you are with me!

I Feast on the Bread of Life

*Blessed shall be your basket
and your kneading bowl.*
DEUTERONOMY 28:5

How I rejoice, Father, that I don't have to worry about inflation, the price of food, and shopping. I praise you that complex economic policies, the rise and fall of the stock market, and business red tape don't have any effect on your blessings. Heavenly Father, when you say my basket is blessed, *it is blessed*! My kneading bowl, or my bread, is blessed because I'm feasting on Jesus—the bread of life! Your blessings come as promises in power and in truth! You are my God. Nations rise and decay under your hand, but your blessings remain with me through thick and thin! Father, I will not worry because I'm too busy praising and thanking you to have time for it!

I Am Blessed
Coming or Going

Blessed shall you be when you come in,
and blessed shall you be when you go out.
DEUTERONOMY 28:6

I'm blessed coming in, and I'm blessed going out!
Father, when I knock on the door, you open it so
I can come in and I am blessed! When I go out to
seek, you help me to find what I'm seeking, and
again, I'm blessed! Father, only through you I am I
assured of getting blessed whether I'm coming or
going! I praise you, heavenly Father, for directing
my way, because in your glorious wisdom, I am
guided to the door of opportunities that bless me.
I am guided out the door to better opportunities
that bless me again. I rejoice and thank you, Father,
that you care for me enough to always bless my
coming in and going out.

My Enemies Are Scattered

The LORD will cause your enemies who rise
against you to be defeated before your face;
they shall come out against you one way
and flee before you seven ways.

DEUTERONOMY 28:7

Enemies, get ready to go! I thank you, Father, that those who come against me with evil in their hearts will never find me alone, but I am always safe with you. I praise you because in your righteousness and power, you defeat my enemies and strike confusion into their ranks so they run before me in seven different ways! Father, even when I am under attack, I'm still blessed because I stand firm and glorify you before the world for causing the defeat of unrighteousness. Thank you, heavenly Father, for blessing me under all conditions! I can't lose with you, Father, because I'm blessed when they attack me, and I'm blessed when they leave me alone!

My Storehouse Is Blessed

The LORD will command the blessing on you in your
storehouses and in all to which you set your hand, and
He will bless you in the land which the LORD your God
is giving you.

DEUTERONOMY 28:8

Everything I undertake is blessed— what a
promise! Father, I praise you because when
you command something to be done, *it is done*!
Thank you for commanding a blessing upon me
personally, for the projects I've already started and
the things I'm going to do in the future. Father,
I work with your praises upon my lips because
you bless and reward those who are faithful to
you. I don't worry about my savings, because your
blessing protects what is mine better than any
bank vault. I'm not anxious about the success of
anything I tackle because under your blessing,
my work prospers! Father, you have blessed me in
everything you have given me, and I am grateful to
you. Hallelujah!

God Honors My Work

And the LORD will grant you plenty of goods, in the fruit of your body, in the increase of your livestock, and in the produce of your ground, in the land of which the LORD swore to your fathers to give you.

DEUTERONOMY 28:11

Thank you, Father, that your Word promises more than bare sufficiency; your Word promises *plenteous goods*! I rejoice and praise you because your plan for me is a life of abundance, not just scraping by day-to-day. I thank you because everything I do multiplies and bears fruit in the power of your generous and loving blessing upon me and upon my land. Father, you are a fountain of blessings to me and I glorify your name! I have more than enough, and I will always have an excess, an oversupply, and a balance left over to give to others in need! Hallelujah!

God Gives from His Treasury

The LORD will open to you
His good treasure.
DEUTERONOMY 28:12

Father, when I think that you open to me your good treasure, I know it means everything you've got is open and available to me. I feel like a child, full of excitement, sticking my hand in a grab bag of goodies! Some things in a grab bag are disappointing, but Father, *all* of the things in your treasury are good! I rejoice because it is truly your pleasure to give me the kingdom. When you open something up, you don't open just a little crack, but you open it wide. I thank you and rejoice that you are the one who's doing it, Father, and that you don't make me try to chisel my way inside of something difficult to get into. You open it up to me—free of charge. How I love you for your generosity!

I Walk in Righteousness

A good man leaves an inheritance to his children's children, but the wealth of the sinner is stored up for the righteous.

PROVERBS 13:22

I glorify you, Father, because you are providing for me a rich inheritance to leave my children and my children's children. My family line will be blessed for every generation until you return because you are blessing me today and guiding me in your paths of righteousness. Heavenly Father, I thank you that I am also leaving an inheritance of moral values and good behavior to my children and my children's children, both through the example I set for them and through teaching them your Word. Father, I lift my hands up right now to be a funnel for you to pour the sinner's wealth into me, and I receive your abundance. Amen!

God Establishes My Plans

Commit your works to the LORD,
and your thoughts will be established.
PROVERBS 16:3

My plans are established and succeeding! What a promise! I praise you, Father, because when I bring my intentions, plans, and ideas to you before I start on any project, you conform my thoughts and will so that everything I do succeeds wonderfully. Even if I come to you with wrong ideas, you roll them all upon you, committing them to your precious care. You turn my thoughts around so that I think in the right direction. I'm letting all of my thoughts go straight to you. Without you, my thoughts could go off track and get me into trouble; but with you, my plans are established and succeeding. Hallelujah!

No Weapon against Me Will Prosper

*"No weapon formed against you shall prosper,
and every tongue which rises against you in judgment
You shall condemn. This is the heritage of the servants
of the LORD, and their righteousness is from Me,"
says the LORD.*

ISAIAH 54:17

Father, I rejoice that my heritage in you protects me from the weapons of enemies and the tongues of the wicked or mistaken people who speak against me. My righteousness is in you, so I have nothing to fear. The devil and his deceptions are turned away from me and are brought to nothing by your power because my faith is in you, and you are my shield and my buckler. Thank you for wrapping your shield of faith around me so that I can confidently face the world and know that no weapon of any kind that is formed against me can prosper in any way because of your Word!

God's Word Has Power

So shall My word be that goes forth from My mouth;
It shall not return to Me void, but it shall accomplish
what I please, and it shall prosper in the thing for
which I sent it.

ISAIAH 55:11

Glory, Father, that your Word goes forth with power and it does what you intend it to do! I thank you because your promises and your blessings prosper me and my works, exactly as you want them to. I thank you for your loving kindness, for the many blessings you have poured out upon me this month, and for your constant presence in my life. I praise you because you are a God of power, glory, and righteousness, and because the Word that goes forth from your mouth with such wonderful authority brings me joy, peace, love, happiness, friendship, health, and prosperity as I let those same words flow through my mouth!

APRIL

The Name of Jesus

Confess the following prayer every day this month, along with the one for each day, to firmly establish in your mind that He is risen:

"Thank you, Father, that we can say Jesus is risen. When they went to the tomb, He was not there! It was empty! Jesus, thank you for dying on the cross and taking all of the sins of mankind upon yourself. You established forever that your name is above all other names when you arose victoriously out of the bonds of hell and over the power of Satan. Thank you, Father, for the resurrection power that made salvation possible."

Each day as you make your declaration, whether you are alone or with someone, say it out loud, and say it with authority until the declaration that is written becomes your declaration! The name of Jesus is above every other name!

I Confess Jesus Is Lord

Therefore God has highly exalted him and bestowed on him the name that is above every name, so that at the name of Jesus every knee should bow, in heaven and on earth and under the earth, and every tongue confess that Jesus Christ is Lord, to the glory of God the Father.
PHILIPPIANS 2:9–11, ESV

Jesus, Jesus, Jesus. How I love that name! I thank you, Father, for giving your Son such a beautiful name. Thank you for your power in that name. I praise you that the name of Jesus is over and above sickness, disease, poverty, demons, and everything else the devil tries to give me. I take the name of Jesus over any plague that tries to come near my dwelling, because that name is above all things inside and out. My tongue confesses daily that Jesus Christ is Lord. Jesus is Lord! *Jesus is Lord*!

My Heart Is Peaceful

Then He arose and rebuked the wind,
and said to the sea, "Peace, be still!"
And the wind ceased and there was a great calm.

MARK 4:39

Father, how we praise you! We know that if we call upon the name of Jesus, the wildest storm that is blowing around us will be still and quiet. When the enemy comes, the name of Jesus muzzles whatever the devil is trying to do. My heart shall have peace all day today because whenever the wind starts to blow, I shall take the name of Jesus on my lips. Thank you for the peace that passes all understanding that rests in my heart because of what you've given to us in the name of Jesus!

I Praise the Name of Jesus

That the name of our Lord Jesus Christ may be glorified in you, and you in Him, according to the grace of our God and the Lord Jesus Christ.

2 THESSALONIANS 1:12

Father, it has been over 2,000 years since you sent your Son to walk on this earth. I can't stop talking about His miraculous life and I can't thank you and praise you enough for sending Him. I thank and praise you for giving me the opportunity to have Jesus glorified in me by the way I live my life before others, and to be glorified, myself, because I live in Him. Thank you, Father, because this can only happen by your grace and that of our Lord Jesus Christ. Thank you for that beautiful name above all names, the name of Jesus! I speak daily in thanksgiving about what you have done for me.

I Am Healed

And the whole multitude sought to touch Him,
for power went out from Him and healed them all.
LUKE 6:19

He healed them all! What a statement, and what
a truth! I praise you and exalt the name of Jesus
because Jesus and His name are one, Father! There
was so much power in His very being, His presence,
that the ever-present virtue flowed out of Him and
healed every person. I thank you because you have
given me the same power and the authority to use
the name of Jesus to let healing virtue flow out
of me. I praise you that Jesus was victorious in all
circumstances and at all times, therefore, because
I am a joint heir with Him, I am victorious and
triumphant at all times because of that name: *Jesus!*
Name above all names!

I Will Ask and Receive

"In that day you will ask nothing of me. Truly, truly,
I say to you, whatever you ask of the Father in my
name, he will give it to you. Until now you have asked
nothing in my name. Ask, and you will receive, that
your joy may be full."

JOHN 16:23–24, ESV

Your goodness is overwhelming. My joy is full
and running all over the place! I thank you, Father,
that Jesus said *whatever* I ask in His *name,* you will
give to me. I rejoice and give thanks that the name
Jesus has such power and authority. I'm blessed to
ask in the name of Jesus because of the love that
fills my heart when His name is on my tongue and
because of the joy of receiving what I ask from you.
Thank you for giving so bountiful in my life that
my joy is running over!

I Bear Good Fruit

You did not choose Me, but I chose you and appointed you that you should go and bear fruit, and that your fruit should remain, that whatever you ask the Father in My name He may give you.
JOHN 15:16

You chose me! You ordained me! You picked me out because you wanted to! I thank you, Father, that I am chosen and ordained through Jesus Christ to bear fruit in my life from the love and truth He expresses in me. Thank you that I live so that people can see the love of Jesus in me and that I can reach out to tell the Good News to others. Thank you that I am appointed to bring forth fruit and that my fruit will remain as your Word says, so that I can ask for anything in Jesus' name and you will give it to me! So I ask that my life will bear much fruit, and that fruit will remain.

I Will Do Greater Works

Very truly I tell you, whoever believes in me will do the works I have been doing, and they will do even greater things than these, because I am going to the Father. And I will do whatever you ask in my name, so that the Father may be glorified in the Son. You may ask me for anything in my name, and I will do it.

JOHN 14:12–14, NIV

I believe in you, Jesus. I get so excited when I read that I can do even greater things than you did. My mind can't comprehend all the things you've promised, but I believe them because you have said so in your Word. I thank you that your Word makes such a complete and total statement. Because you picked the word *whatever*, I know that if I asked in the name of Jesus, it will be done! Father, I want to glorify your Son in all that I do! I'm walking in power because you said so!

I Receive the Holy Spirit

*Peter said to them, "Repent, and each of you
be baptized in the name of Jesus Christ for the
forgiveness of your sins; and you will receive the gift
of the Holy Spirit."*
ACTS 2:38, NASB

Father, I rejoice and thank you for the power that's in the name of Jesus! I thank you that at with your name, the lame shall walk, the blind shall see, and healings shall take place today just as they did in the days when the disciples walked on this earth. I thank you for the blessings that the name of Jesus brings. I thank you for the gift of the Holy Spirit. Thank you for the power that comes with the Holy Spirit. Thank you for the joy that comes with the Holy Spirit. I praise you, Father, that you give *all* of your blessings to *all* of your children. I'm not going to miss a single one!

I Speak a Heavenly Language

And these signs will follow those who believe:
In My name they will cast out demons;
they will speak with new tongues.

MARK 16:17

Glorious Father, how I praise and thank you that in the name of Jesus I have power over devils. They all know who Jesus is, and I don't have to fear them one bit because the devil himself trembles at the very name of Jesus! Thank you, Father, that all the powers of darkness are afraid and run away at the mention of Jesus, because through Him, they and every evil plan are defeated. What a blessing you give to us, Jesus, when we speak with new tongues. Thank you, Father, for the language of love you give us with which to praise you and love you. Thank you that this is for all believers, and that includes me! Thank you for these signs!

I Have Healing Hands

They will be able to handle snakes with safety, and if they drink anything poisonous, it won't hurt them. They will be able to place their hands on the sick, and they will be healed.

MARK 16:18

Thank you, Father, that as I look at my hands I don't see anything supernatural. I don't see anything unusual; I don't see much of anything except fingers on each hand. But your Word says that in the name of Jesus, these ordinary hands can be laid on sick people and *they will recover!* I praise you for not saying maybe, or that only some would be used, but you just simply said that the hands of believers would be used! I'm a believer, Father, and even though I might not be able to feel power flowing through my hands at all times, by faith in your Word, I know it's there, and I know that the sick will recover when my hands are laid upon them! Thank you that my family is made whole by the use of my hands!

I Boldly Believe God

So they called them and commanded them not to speak at all nor teach in the name of Jesus. ... Saying, "Did we not strictly command you not to teach in this name? And look, you have filled Jerusalem with your doctrine, and intend to bring this Man's blood on us!" But Peter and the other apostles answered and said: "We ought to obey God rather than men."

ACTS 4:18, 5:28–29

Thank you, Father, that the name of Jesus has so much power that the devil and his cohorts flee at the very mention of His name. People were so afraid at the mention of the name of Jesus they forbade Peter and John to ever speak of His name. Thank you for their boldness in saying, "We ought to obey God rather than men." I praise you that I can use that same boldness today, say the exact same words, and be a God-pleaser and not a people-pleaser. Thank you for the power in Jesus' name.

I Praise God's Glorious Name

And those who went before
and those who followed
were shouting, "Hosanna!
Blessed is he who comes in the name of the Lord!"

MARK 11:9, ESV

Father, I thank you that I come in the name of the Lord, because I am a child of God, redeemed by the blood of the Lamb, the sacrifice of Jesus Christ on the cross, and because of the word of my testimony. I rejoice and praise you, Father, that because I come in His name, I am blessed. Thank you for sending your Son, Jesus, to prepare the way for us to follow Him. I'm singing and shouting His praises because I come in His name!

God's Word Is Eternal

Heaven and earth will pass away,
but My words will by no means pass away.
MATTHEW 24:35

Father, it is beyond my comprehension that this earth will some day pass away, and that the sun, moon, and stars that I've seen and been used to all my life will pass away. But I believe it because your Word says so! I rejoice that the things of your eternal kingdom shall not pass away, and that you have chosen me to spend eternity in your glorious kingdom because of my salvation in Jesus Christ! How I thank you for sending your Son, and praise you for your Word in which I will stand on all the days of my life. It lifts my spirit up to the heavenly places when I think of these wonderful promises!

I Walk in Authority

*Behold, I give you the authority to trample
on serpents and scorpions,
and over all the power of the enemy,
and nothing shall by any means hurt you.*

LUKE 10:19

That is real power, Father! I thank you because
Jesus unreservedly gave me the power to walk on
things that would seek to harm me. I thank you
that this power was magnified to give me power
over all the enemy, without possibility of retaliation
upon me, because Jesus guaranteed that nothing
would be able by any means to hurt me. I praise
you, Father, because Jesus didn't limit my power
to particular conditions, and didn't say I only
have power over part of the enemy, but over *all* the
enemy's power! Thank you, Father, that nothing is
going to hurt me because Jesus gave me that power
in His name!

God Guides the Way

Assuredly, I say to you, whoever does not receive the kingdom of God as a little child will by no means enter it.

LUKE 18:17

Glory, Father! I'm so thankful because getting into your kingdom is so simple that I'm going to shout out your praises! What a blessing that I am not required to have a college degree. I don't even have to speak Greek or Hebrew, and I don't have to belong to a certain club or be an expert in anything. I'm so glad that you let me join your special club just by simple faith in the blood of Jesus. I didn't gain access by intellect, meditation, or muscles. There wasn't anything to figure out. I didn't have to buy a ticket and there was no red tape. How I praise you, Father, that you sent Jesus to show me the way! I humbly and gratefully receive your wonderful gift.

God Makes the Impossible Possible

But He said,
"The things which are impossible with men
are possible with God."

LUKE 18:27

I will not be limited by what others say can or cannot be done. I praise you, Father, because there is an infinitely greater hope, an infinitely greater power than what man or science says I can do. Because Jesus said it, it became so! Those very things, which are impossible with men, are possible with you. Thank you, Father, that through you I can expect the impossible and the miraculous to happen! You are the changeless God! You are the same God of miracles today as you were 2,000 years ago, or in Moses' time, or at creation! I am glad that you are *my* Father!

I Am Found

For the Son of Man has come to seek and to save that which was lost.
LUKE 19:10

He searched for me. He hunted me. He pursued me. He sought me! Thank you, Father, for sending your very own Son, Jesus, to rescue me when I was lost in the darkness of sin. I thank you that you loved me so much, you let your own Son bear my sins upon the cross, so that I might be cleansed and saved from eternal damnation. I was lost, but He found me and saved me so I could become part of your kingdom! I rejoice that Jesus shined His light on the path that led me right to your gate! Father, I will praise you and glorify your name forever that your Son was sacrificed so I could have eternal life! I thank you that you are seeking to save all that which is lost—every person, every thing—and that everyone I know and love will come to know you and enter your kingdom. Thank you, Father!

God's Joy Makes Me Strong

Do not sorrow,
for the joy of the Lord is your strength.
NEHEMIAH 8:10

Jesus gives joy! Glory to God! I sing hosanna to the highest because of the joy that overflows in my heart. I praise you that the redeemed of the Lord shall return and come with singing unto Zion, and everlasting joy shall be upon their heads. How I praise you that they shall obtain gladness and joy, and sorrow and sighing shall flee away. I can rejoice because my name is written in heaven. Father, I thank you for the beautiful words of the angel when he said, "Behold, I bring you good tidings of great joy!" (Luke 2:10). Thank you that the Good News was Jesus and the good tidings still bring joy today. Father, I'm walking and leaping and praising you because of the overabundance of joy in my heart! And that joy is my strength.

I Am Free from Sin and Death

Therefore if the Son makes you free,
you shall be free indeed.

JOHN 8:36

Most assuredly, I say to you,
if anyone keeps My word
he shall never see death.

JOHN 8:51

I'm free, I'm free, I'm free indeed. I am liberated. I am unconditionally set free! I am unquestionably set free because Jesus set me free. Father, I thank you for the freedom I have in this beautiful country of mine, but I thank you much more for the freedom Jesus came to bring me! Thank you that you sent Jesus to free me from bondage to sin and to free me from death, which your Word says is the wages of sin. I rejoice and praise your name, Father, because now I shall never see spiritual death! I have a glorious eternal life ahead of me, and I'm enjoying it this very minute! Thank you, Father! Hallelujah!

I Live in Abundance

The thief comes only to steal and kill and destroy.
I came that they may have life and have it abundantly.
JOHN 10:10, ESV

The devil is good for nothing! He steals, he robs, he plunders, he hijacks, he swindles, he blackmails, he cheats, and he tries to destroy everything that comes his way! Father, how I love you that Jesus came to give me the abundant life by restoring me to your love, the source of all abundance! I thank you that the devil who comes as a thief, is powerless to steal the new life I have in you because he has to run from the very name of Jesus! Thank you, Father, for my new life of abundance—love, joy, health, abundance, and eternal life in your kingdom! Hallelujah!

My Seeds Produce a Harvest

Most assuredly, I say to you, unless a grain of wheat falls into the ground and dies, it remains alone; but if it dies, it produces much grain.

JOHN 12:24

I see a whole wheat field, Father, swaying in the breeze of the Holy Spirit. How I thank you that Jesus died on the cross and rose again the third day, to bring forth the fruit of salvation in me so I could have eternal life in your kingdom! I thank you that I'm part of that fruit crop! If that one kernel had not died, Father, there would have never been a way for me to have eternal life. My sins were washed away in the blood of the Lamb you sent as a living sacrifice for me! I rejoice because I'm a new person living a new life in your love, and all of this was made possible through one precious kernel—your lovely Son Jesus!

I Am Sanctified and Justified

And such were some of you. But you were washed, but you were sanctified, but you were justified in the name of the Lord Jesus and by the Spirit of our God.
1 CORINTHIANS 6:11

Father, I praise you that I have been washed absolutely clean and spotless and purified by the blood of Jesus, which has provided complete atonement for my sin. I have been set free from the guilt of sin, and I am set apart, consecrated, purified, sanctioned, and authorized in that name that is above all names! I praise you that I have been pronounced righteous, and all the things that you held against me before I was saved are now just as if they had never happened. I take that wonderful name upon my lips at all times and tell the world about the wonderful things that happen in that name!

I Have Divine Peace

Peace I leave with you, My peace I give to you;
not as the world gives do I give to you.
Let not your heart be troubled,
neither let it be afraid.

JOHN 14:27

Your peace certainly is different from the world, Father! I rejoice and thank you for that very special kind of peace that Jesus gives to me. I praise you that I don't have to be agitated and disturbed by happenings in the world because that's not the kind of peace you give. That special peace is a divine peace that calms my heart and mind in exactly the same manner Jesus did when He commanded a storm to cease when His disciples in the boat became afraid. I praise you, Father, that nothing and no one can ever trouble my heart or take away the peace that Jesus gave me, because it's divine, and it's mine!

I Abide in God's Love

If you abide in Me,
and My words abide in you,
you will ask what you desire,
and it shall be done for you.

JOHN 15:7

Jesus, I'm abiding in you! I'm vitally united to you through your Word, and I'm letting your words settle down deep inside of me, into all the dark corners of my life so that they will permanently dwell, reside, live, and stay within me at all times. I'm speaking your words. I'm living your words. I'm loving your words! I'm blessed and thankful to be always with you and your abiding love, to be able to ask *anything* of you and know that it will be done. Father, I praise you and bless you because you are always there to provide answers to my problems, to love me and nourish me and lift me up! I'm soaring higher all the time because I'm abiding in you and you're abiding in me!

I Have the Hope of Glory

To them God has chosen to make known among
the Gentiles the glorious riches of this mystery,
which is Christ in you, the hope of glory.
COLOSSIANS 1:27

Thank you, Father, that you have made known to me what was once a mystery to the Gentiles— that Jesus Christ lives right inside me! I praise you because with Jesus, I have the riches of glory, the power to live righteously in this world, and the hope of eternal life in your kingdom! Thank you, Father, that it pleases you to make this mystery known to me, so I can live by faith in your grace through Jesus Christ, and let my light shine before mankind! I don't know how He does it, Father, and that's not important! The important thing is that He does!

I Am Made in the Image of God

*And have put on the new self, which is being
renewed in knowledge in the image of its Creator. ...
Therefore, as God's chosen people, holy and dearly
loved, clothe yourselves with compassion, kindness,
humility, gentleness and patience.*

COLOSSIANS 3:10,12, NIV

Father, thank you that I am a new person in
Christ, with a new spiritual self that is continually
renewed and perfected in knowledge, after the
image of my Creator. Thank you that I'm being
sanctified and made holy as one of your elect. To
do your works I've been given your characteristics—
mercy, kindness, humility, meekness, patience,
and willingness to endure whatever comes before
me. Thank you, Father, for your love, because these
things would never be mine in the flesh, but they
are mine because of you.

I Am Holy and Set Apart

For God did not call us to uncleanness,
but in holiness.
1 THESSALONIANS 4:7

I praise you, Father, for your Word, which speaks loud and clear. My calling is not just a part-time job where I can do your holy work part of the time and fool around with sin at other times. Thank you that you want me all of me all the time! I praise you that I don't have unclean desires and thoughts because you protect and shield me from the filth that the devil throws at me. Thank you, Father, as I follow Jesus Christ and abide in Him, that the power of righteousness now flows through me and I am victorious in Christ!

I Have Divine Wisdom

If any of you lacks wisdom, let him ask of God,
who gives to all liberally and without reproach,
and it will be given to him. But let him ask in faith,
with no doubting, for he who doubts is like a wave
of the sea driven and tossed by the wind.

JAMES 1:5–6

Father, I thank you for all the things I can ask in the name of Jesus. Thank you for telling me that if I lack wisdom, all I have to do is ask and it is mine, given liberally without question. I rejoice in the strength of faith I have to ask and receive from you, and I thank you that I'm not blown this and that way like a weather vane. Thank you, Father, that my faith is steady and constant. I really appreciate that even though I might be very deficient in natural wisdom, because I have asked, I have received divine wisdom because I have the mind of Christ!

I Draw Near to God

Submit yourselves therefore to God. Resist the devil, and he will flee from you. Draw near to God, and he will draw near to you. Cleanse your hands, you sinners, and purify your hearts, you double-minded.

JAMES 4:7–8, ESV

Devil, I'm resisting you, and you will flee from me! Thank you, Father, that I can come before you with clean hands and a pure heart. I submit myself completely to you, giving thanks because as I draw near to you, you come closer and closer to me. I praise you, Father, that I have power not only to resist the devil, but to chase him away completely. He has to flee before your power. No longer will I be double-minded with wavering and divided interests, but I shall be single-minded, desiring only to serve and love you! The devil can't touch me!

I Was Made with Purpose on Purpose

For if you remain completely silent at this time, relief and deliverance will arise for the Jews from another place, but you and your father's house will perish. Yet who knows whether you have come to the kingdom for such a time as this?

ESTHER 4:14

Father, you sent your Son to this world at just the right time, and you brought me into this world for such a time as this. Thank you that your timing is perfect in all things. I am excited about that day when your perfect timing will close the world as I know it today. In the midst of the world's failing systems, thank you that I stand on that solid rock of Jesus! You will bring relief and deliverance to others through my life. I am available, Father, and I glory in your perfect timing!

MAY

Blessings

God loves us so much that His heart cries when we don't avail ourselves of all the blessings He wants to give us. Look how easy He makes it for us:

Christ has redeemed us from the curse of the law, having become a curse for us (for it is written, "Cursed is everyone who hangs on a tree"), that the blessing of Abraham might come upon the Gentiles in Christ Jesus, that we might receive the promise of the Spirit through faith ... And if you are Christ's, then you are Abraham's seed, and heirs according to the promise (Galatians 3:13–14, 29).

Every blessing that belonged to Abraham belongs to you and to me. Hallelujah!

I Walk with the Righteous

Blessed is the man who walks not in the counsel of the ungodly, nor stands in the path of sinners, nor sits in the seat of the scornful; but his delight is in the law of the LORD, and in His law he meditates day and night. He shall be like a tree planted by the rivers of water, that brings forth its fruit in its season, whose leaf also shall not wither; and whatever he does shall prosper.

PSALM 1:1–3

Father, I'm blessed, blessed, blessed! I'm happy, fortunate, and prosperous because I don't follow the advice, plans, or purposes of the ungodly. Just lead them to me and I'll share the Good News. I certainly am not going to sit down with the scoffers and mockers, but I constantly meditate in your laws and your words. Your promises are music to my ears and sweet as honey in my mouth. I thank you that everything I do in you prospers in a marvelous way because my joy is in your law.

God Is My Shepherd

The LORD is my shepherd; I shall not want.
He makes me to lie down in green pastures;
He leads me beside the still waters.
He restores my soul;
He leads me in the paths of righteousness
for His name's sake.

PSALM 23:1–3

I lack nothing in my life, Father, because you lead me to beautiful places where I am nourished and at peace, both physically and spiritually. Father, I praise you and thank you for that, because you are my shepherd, my light, and my hope. You feed and clothe me and restore my soul when I'm weary because you love me as a shepherd loves his flock. I thank you that whenever I'm rushing around too much, you lead me beside the still waters, out of the turmoil of life. Thank you, Father, for protecting me from the wolves of the world and for leading me in the paths of righteousness.

God Prepares a Table for Me

Yea, though I walk through the valley of the shadow of death, I will fear no evil; For You are with me; Your rod and Your staff, they comfort me. You prepare a table before me in the presence of my enemies; You anoint my head with oil; My cup runs over.

PSALM 23:4–5

Father, thank you that I don't walk into the valley of the shadow of death and sit down. No, you've said that I walk *through* the deep, sunless valley of the shadow of death. Hallelujah, I'm walking right out of that valley whether it be sickness, poverty, or depression, and I fear no evil because *you* protect me. Thank you for preparing a spiritual feast for me right in front of my enemies!

My Head Is Anointed

You anoint my head with oil; My cup runs over. Surely goodness and mercy shall follow me all the days of my life; and I will dwell in the house of the LORD Forever.

PSALM 23:5–6

How I rejoice, Father, that I'm so blessed, because you anoint my head with so much of the oil of the Holy Spirit that my cup runs over. You don't give me just a little trickle; you give me a cup that runs and runs and runs over! Thank you, Father, because two things are going to follow me all the days of my life: goodness and mercy! Not sorrow and sadness, but goodness and mercy, and I thank you because I'm blessed to be able to dwell in the house of the Lord forever!

My Sin Is Forgiven

Blessed is he whose transgression is forgiven,
whose sin is covered.
PSALM 32:1

I'm blessed! I'm happy! I'm fortunate! I'm to be envied! All because my sins are forgiven! My sins are covered by your precious blood in such a way that you can't even see them. I'm walking on air because a huge burden has been lifted from my shoulders and replaced by that wonderful blessing because *all* my sins are gone. How I thank you that the blood of Jesus was sufficient to cover the sins of the whole world, including mine, and I praise you that when you forgive sins you also forget them. I'm a brand new person to you. Thank you for the tremendous and unending supply of love you've poured out on me!

I Delight Myself in God

Delight yourself also in the Lord,
and He shall give you the desires of your heart.
Commit your way to the Lord, trust also in Him,
and He shall bring it to pass.

PSALM 37:4–5

I delighted in you and with you, Lord, and my heart is overflowing with good measure. You see deep and directly into my heart, and you give me the desires of my heart because you have taken out the carnal desires of the flesh I once had, and you have replaced them with your divine desires. You even grant those secret requests that no one knows about except you and me. Since I've committed my life to you and trust you completely, you give me what I desire, the best things, not substitutes or imitations. No one has a better father than I do, because *you* are my Father, and your promises stagger my wildest imagination. Hallelujah! I'm blessed because you're bringing good things to pass! Glory!

God's Mercy Endures Forever

Oh, give thanks to the Lord, for He is good!
For His mercy endures forever.
Oh, give thanks to the God of gods!
For His mercy endures forever.
Oh, give thanks to the Lord of lords!
For His mercy endures forever.
Read the rest of Psalm 136 and
then make the following declaration:

Heavenly Father, I'm blessed because you are a good God and your mercy endures forever. I've committed sins, but in your mercy you have forgiven them. You've given me a beautiful world in which to live. Because of your mercy, you have given me friends who delight my heart and you've kept my enemies off my back. You didn't have to do any of these things for me, but you did, because of your mercy. Thank you, Father, that your loving kindness and mercy will continue unceasingly and eternally!

God Never Leaves Me

You have hedged me behind and before, and laid Your hand upon me. Such knowledge is too wonderful for me; it is high, I cannot attain it. Where can I go from your Spirit? Or where can I flee from Your presence? If I ascend into heaven, You are there; if I make my bed in hell, behold, You are there. If I take the wings of the morning, and dwell in the uttermost parts of the sea, even there Your hand shall lead me, and Your right hand shall hold me.

PSALM 139:5–10

Father, I'm blessed by your glorious presence wherever I go, whether I'm in Arkansas, New York, Zambia, or China. If I were an astronaut, Father, I'd find you in outer space. I rejoice in the blessing of your presence from which I never want to depart, for it's your hand that guides me along the straight and narrow path. Thank you, Lord, for your presence in my life. Thank you that I can never be lost to your sight!

God Is My Rock

Blessed be the LORD, my rock, who trains my hands for war, and my fingers for battle; he is my steadfast love and my fortress, my stronghold and my deliverer, my shield and he in whom I take refuge, who subdues people under me.

PSALM 144:1–2, ESV

Father, I'm blessed because your keen strength and supreme power protect me under all conditions no matter how difficult they look. I'm blessed, too, because your strength makes me a spiritual warrior armed with the razor-sharp sword of your righteousness, so that I actively take part in the war against darkness. I'm blessed because you never leave me nor forsake me and your steadfast love surrounds me at all times. You are my high tower of safety, my deliverer, and my shield to protect me from the darts of the devil at all times, and you subdue those enemies who try to attack me! I glory in such a glorious God!

God Gives Me Spiritual Blessings

Blessed be the God and Father of our Lord Jesus Christ, who has blessed us with every spiritual blessing in the heavenly places in Christ.

EPHESIANS 1:3

All spiritual blessings in heavenly places are mine! I give you praise and adoration because you are the Father of our Lord Jesus Christ, the Messiah. I rejoice that Jesus is with you in heaven and is preparing a place for me there. I'm ready for that wonderful day when He will come to take me home to you. In the meantime, I'm going to enjoy all the Holy-Spirit-given blessings in heaven and earth that you've passed on to us through your wonderful Son! Glory!

The Blessings of Abraham Are on Me

But Christ has rescued us from the curse pronounced by the law. When he was hung on the cross, he took upon himself the curse for our wrongdoing. For it is written in the Scriptures, "Cursed is everyone who is hung on a tree." Through Christ Jesus, God has blessed the Gentiles with the same blessing he promised to Abraham, so that we who are believers might receive the promised Holy Spirit through faith. ... And now that you belong to Christ, you are the true children of Abraham. You are his heirs, and God's promise to Abraham belongs to you.

GALATIANS 3:13–14, 29

I'm redeemed by the blood of the Lamb! I've been redeemed from the curse of the law because of Jesus Christ. Thank you for sending my Lord Jesus to wash my sins away and remove the curse that separates me from you and your love. Your love lifts and blesses me constantly. Thank you, Father, for your endless blessings and for making me an heir to all the promises of Abraham. I am a part of your family!

—

I Will Reap a Good Harvest

Do not be deceived: God cannot be mocked. A man reaps what he sows. Whoever sows to please their flesh, from the flesh will reap destruction; whoever sows to please the Spirit, from the Spirit will reap eternal life.

GALATIANS 6:7–8

I'm overcome with blessings today, Father, because you've promised that whatever we sow, we shall reap. I'm sowing a bumper crop of love, joy, and peace today, Father. I'm not planting my seed in the infertile soil of the flesh because I don't want to reap corruption; I'm sowing to the spirit to be able to reap life everlasting! I praise you that my life is not down here, but my real life is in heaven with you and Jesus! I'm blessed because you make this all possible for me personally, and how I love you for that!

I Am Saved by Grace and Faith

And raised us up together, and made us sit together in the heavenly places in Christ Jesus, that in the ages to come He might show the exceeding riches of His grace in His kindness toward us in Christ Jesus. For by grace you have been saved through faith, and that not of yourselves; it is the gift of God, not of works, lest anyone should boast.

EPHESIANS 2:6–9

Glory to God, you've raised me up, and I'm sitting in heavenly places in Christ Jesus. I love you for that. Thank you, Father, that my salvation is not dependent upon my good works, but is entirely dependent upon the exceeding riches of your grace. You so simply said if I would believe in Jesus Christ, His work at Calvary, His blood, and confess it with my mouth, I would be saved. Hallelujah, Father, I'm saved and filled with your love! I can't boast about it, either, because you did it all!

God Dwells in Me

That Christ may dwell in your hearts through faith;
that you, being rooted and grounded in love, may be
able to comprehend with all the saints what is the
width and length and depth and height— to know the
love of Christ which passes knowledge; that you may be
filled with all the fullness of God.

EPHESIANS 3:17–19

Thank you, Father, for blessing me with the knowledge that Christ lives in my heart because I trust in Him. I am rooted and firmly grounded in that tremendous love, which is so long, so wide, so high, and so deep that I will never really be able to understand the greatness of this love for me. Thank you, Father, for the knowledge that some day I will be filled with you! What a promise! I don't deserve it, but I receive it!

I Wear the Full Armor of God

Finally, be strong in the Lord and in his mighty power. Put on the full armor of God, so that you can take your stand against the devil's schemes.
EPHESIANS 6:10-11, NIV

I praise you, Father, for blessing me with your strength, and the power of your might! Because you provided my whole armor, it is invincible, unconquerable, unyielding, and indomitable! I am blessed because even though I don't wrestle against flesh and blood, but against principalities, against powers, against the rulers of the darkness of this world, and against spiritual wickedness in high places, you have given me your whole armor to wear for protection. With the power of your might going before me, Father, I will always be victorious!

God Keeps His Promises

Praise the LORD who has given rest to his people Israel, just as he promised. Not one word has failed of all the wonderful promises he gave through his servant Moses.

1 KINGS 8:56

What a blessing it is to serve you, Father. When the world lies, cheats, and fails to keep its word, you are always right there, fulfilling all of your promises. Thank you that the God of Abraham, Isaac, and Jacob knows my name too! Thank you for being a God of integrity, Father, so that I can be an imitator of you and be a person of integrity in all of my dealings. Thank you that all of the blessings of Abraham are mine because your Word promises this; you never fail to keep your promises. Hallelujah, what a God I serve! I'm blessed!

I Am Fruitful

Then God blessed them and said, "Be fruitful and multiply. Fill the earth and govern it. Reign over the fish in the sea, the birds in the sky, and all the animals that scurry along the ground."

GENESIS 1:28, NLT

Father, I'm being overtaken and overcome with blessing, again, because of your love. I'm blessed. I'm blessed because I have dominion over the fish of the sea, over the fowl of the air, and all living things! I'm blessed because I can be used to multiply your family. I'm blessed because I am fruitful. I'm blessed because I was made in your likeness. I'm blessed because this blessing is upon both man and woman alike, in whom there is no difference in your sight. Glory!

—

I Walk in God's Blessings

Arise, walk in the land
through its length and its width,
for I give it to you.
GENESIS 13:17

Father, what blessings you give me. Thank you for the privilege of knowing that all the blessings you bestowed in the beginning of creation have flowed down, through time, to me. Thank you for letting me walk through the length and breadth of the land you have for me, knowing that you will give it to me. Thank you for blessing those who bless me and who bring happiness upon me. Thank you that I can be a blessing also to others by dispensing good to them. Thank you for giving me so much land and possessions that I can share generously with others! How I bless you for all your blessings! I'm walking forward, backward, and sideways over the land you give to me!

God Remains Forever Faithful

Jesus Christ is the same yesterday,
today, and forever.
HEBREWS 13:8

Father, I praise and thank you that your Son alone, among all the constant changes taking place in the world, always remains the same. I thank you that because of this, He still saves, heals, and delivers. You are the living cornerstone of my life, and I am saved, healed, and delivered because He hasn't changed one single bit and never will! I thank you that when the price of gold soars to new highs or drops to new lows that Jesus is exactly the same. Thank you for blessing me with a changeless Savior, my healer, my doorway into your marvelous glorious presence. He is my rock, and I can rely on His sameness forever.

I Am Patient

Therefore be patient, brethren, until the coming of the Lord. See how the farmer waits for the precious fruit of the earth, waiting patiently for it until it receives the early and latter rain.

JAMES 5:7

Heavenly Father, thank you for the blessed hope I have in the coming of my Lord Jesus Christ. I'm blessed now, Father, because He lives in my heart, waiting for exactly the chosen day to come to me in person. Thank you for your Word, Father, which tells me that Christ is like the farmer who waits for the seasonal rains to bring His crop to ripeness before the harvest time. I praise you, Father, for patiently perfecting me in your love so I'll be joyously prepared for that great day! Hallelujah!

God's Word Is Inside Me

*For you have been born again, not of perishable
seed, but of imperishable, through the living and
enduring word of God. For, "All people are like grass,
and all their glory is like the flowers of the field; the
grass withers and the flowers fall, but the word of the
Lord endures forever." And this is the word that was
preached to you.*

1 PETER 1:23–25

Father, I'm born again and I'm filled with your
joy. The incorruptible seed of your Word has been
planted in my heart and is growing every day!
I praise you, Father, that although the things of
this world come and go, your Word, a priceless
eternal treasure, endures forever. Thank you for the
blessing of your living, enduring Word! You are not
temporary; you are eternal, everlasting, and never
wear out!

I Am Blessed
with Eternal Life

*For God so loved the world that He gave His only
begotten Son, that whoever believes in Him should not
perish but have everlasting life.*

JOHN 3:16

Thank you, Father, that because of your love I can
answer my phone and say, "God loves you!" and feel
your love going right through that phone to the
person on the other end. Thank you, Father, that
you love us so much, your imperishable blessings
are available to us. Thank you that I am blessed
because you loved me enough to send your only
begotten Son, Jesus, to die for me so that I might
have eternal life! I love you, Father! I believe and
am grateful for everlasting life.

I Proclaim God's Praises

*But you are a chosen generation, a royal priesthood,
a holy nation, His own special people, that you may
proclaim the praises of Him who called you out of
darkness into His marvelous light.*

1 PETER 2:9

I'm glad I'm different and unique! I'm blessed to belong to a chosen race, a royal priesthood, a holy nation, a member of your own purchased, special people. I can set forth and show to all the world your wonderful deeds and display the virtues and perfections of your divine nature. You have gifted me to minister to the spiritual needs of those around me. My Lord is King of kings and Lord of lords, who has the power to call whosoever He will out of the darkness and death into the marvelous light of new life. Thank you, Father, for giving me the blessing of Jesus and your love in Him. I'm peculiar and I want the world to know the reason for it! Hallelujah!

God Hears My Prayers

For the eyes of the Lord are on the righteous,
and his ears are open to their prayer.
But the face of the Lord is against those who do evil.
1 PETER 3:12

Hallelujah, I can't hide from you, Father. I'm so blessed that your eyes are upon the righteous, those who are in right standing with you. Your Word says that you are attentive and sensitive to my prayers. I'm blessed because your ears are open to me twenty-four hours a day. How I praise you for never tiring of listening to me. Thank you that I am never lost to your sight, but under your tender, loving care at all times. How I praise you that you differentiate between the evil and the righteous because I would never want to have you turn your face from me! I'm never going to even try to hide from you!

I Am Pleasing to God

And whatever we ask we receive from Him,
because we keep His commandments
and do those things that are pleasing in His sight.
1 JOHN 3:22

Whatever I ask is mine because I keep your commands and am pleasing in your sight! What a promise, Father! I'm blessed because you've given me instructions for life that are written down in a book that I can refer to constantly. You shower me with so much love that I rejoice to obey everything you tell me to do! You bless me with your faithfulness, so I bless you with mine! I watchfully and carefully obey all your instructions and do the things that are pleasing in your sight. I observe your suggestions and constantly practice what is pleasing to you. I thank you for being willing to do whatever I ask because my wishes are in line with what you want for me! I'm sailing in blessings!

I Overcome Fear with Faith

There is no fear in love: but perfect love
casts out fear, because fear involves torment.
But he who fears has not been made perfect in love.
1 JOHN 4:18

Father, I'm blessed that I have no fear in me whatsoever because I'm protected by your power and strength from all the things of the devil. By your Word, I have no fear in me and dread does not exist. Your full-blown, perfect love turns fear away from me and gets rid of every trace of terror. I'm blessed, Father, and I praise you that I'm not suffering the torment of darkness because you've lifted me into the wonderful light and complete perfection of your love. Thank you, Father, for blessing me! Regardless of the circumstances, your love overcomes all fear!

God Sends Ministering Angels for Me

Are they not all ministering spirits sent forth to minister for those who will inherit salvation?
HEBREWS 1:14

Thank you, Father, for sending out your angels who are ministering for us constantly because we are heirs of salvation. Thank you, Father, for blessing us with the knowledge that those same angels are bringing our loved ones to that person who will minister salvation to them. Thank you that you send angels forth even without me knowing about it. Thank you for letting them minister for my protection in times of trouble. They keep my foot from slipping when the path gets dangerous. Thank you that your angels can even close the mouths of lions so that they are not a danger to a child of God. I'm blessed because of angels!

I Receive the Spirit of Wisdom and Revelation

I keep asking that the God of our Lord Jesus Christ, the glorious Father, may give you the Spirit of wisdom and revelation, so that you may know him better. I pray that the eyes of your heart may be enlightened in order that you may know the hope to which he has called you, the riches of his glorious inheritance in his holy people.

EPHESIANS 1:17–18, NIV

Glory, Father, for your blessings are overwhelming me with joy. You have granted me a spirit of wisdom, revelation, and insight into mysteries and secrets in the deep and intimate knowledge of your Son. You have flooded the eyes of my heart with light, giving me the privilege of understanding what is the hope of my calling and the riches that are the glorious inheritance of your set-apart ones! I'm blessed because of the magnitude of your blessings!

God's Generosity Is Displayed in My Life

For you know the grace of our Lord Jesus Christ,
that though He was rich, yet for your sakes He became
poor, that you through His poverty might become rich.
2 CORINTHIANS 8:9

Father, your blessings stagger my imagination! I am overwhelmed when I consider that Jesus had everything in your kingdom with all its riches and glories for Himself, yet, He chose to become poor for my sake that I could become rich in you. I praise you that I have been delivered from the curse through Him. I bless you that I am saved through grace because there is no way I could have earned the gift Jesus gave me. It was His kindness and His gracious generosity that make this all possible. I thank you that because of His poverty, I have become enriched and abundantly supplied at all times! I thank you that I am progressively becoming acquainted with these blessings more and more all the time!

My Focus Is Steady

So we fix our eyes not on what is seen,
but on what is unseen,
since what is seen is temporary,
but what is unseen is eternal.
2 CORINTHIANS 4:18, NIV

Thank you, Father, for giving me spiritual eyes so that I don't have to look and see things the way the world sees them. I can look at them through your eyes. Thank you that I don't have to see only the things which are visible to our human eyes, but I can see with my spiritual eyes the glorious things of your kingdom, which is my inheritance. I praise you for this great blessing! I bless you because even though I've never seen you, I *know* you're there at all times, loving and protecting me.

I Live in the Fullness of God

*Beware lest anyone cheat you through philosophy
and empty deceit, according to the tradition of men,
according to the basic principles of the world,
and not according to Christ. For in Him dwells
all the fullness of the Godhead bodily.*

COLOSSIANS 2:8–9

Father, what an overwhelming thought to know
that I am in Christ and He is in me. All the treasures
of divine wisdom and all the riches of spiritual
knowledge and enlightenment are stored up and are
hidden in Him, and they are mine. I have everything
because I am joined with Jesus Christ in salvation.
Father, the world can't talk me out of what your
Word says is mine! My joy and my faith are at an
all-time high because they stand on what Christ
has said. I don't look to the world for their shallow
answers and intellectualism. I look to the Holy Spirit
for my answers to life. Bless you, Father, that you tell
me with no qualms that Jesus is the highest ruler!
Not only that, He is mine! Hallelujah, therefore I
have everything I need in Christ Jesus!

JUNE

Love

Love is our declaration for the month, and what an appropriate subject for the month of June when people think of love and marriage. The love of God for humans, and humans for God, is the most beautiful love in all the world. It is this love that makes us lovable to the world and makes it possible for us to love them. God loves to hear you tell Him how much you love Him, so say it every day, will you?

On June 11, we have asked you to pick out someone to love in a special way. Write and tell us what happened to you and to them (www.joanhunter.org), because of this special day of giving love!

If you want to see some problems disappear in a hurry, write all the problems you have on a piece of paper, and at the bottom write: *"Yet in all these things we are more than conquerors through Him who loved us"* (Romans 8:37). Confess it every day until you discover that every single one of those problems is conquered!

I Am Overflowing with Joy

As the Father loved Me, I also have loved you; abide in My love. If you keep My commandments, you will abide in My love, just as I have kept My Father's commandments and abide in His love. These things I have spoken to you, that My joy may remain in you, and that your joy may be full.

JOHN 15:9-11

My joy is running over and spilling all over the place! Thank you, Father, that in the same way you loved Jesus, He has also loved me. Thank you, Jesus, that because I keep your commandments, I abide in your love all the time. I can abide in your love twenty-four hours a day because your source never runs out and is always available to me. Thank you that my joy is full and running over. Thank you that you gave your joy not as a temporary thing, but as a permanent, full-time gift. Your joy, happiness, and excitement remains in me and is full, complete, and overflowing at all times.

—

I Am Overflowing with Love

Jesus answered and said to him,
"If anyone loves Me, he will keep My word;
and My Father will love him,
and We will come to him
and make Our home with him."
JOHN 14:23

Jesus, I declare that I love you! Father, thank you that your Son is so full of grace. Thank you that I can love Him at all times and keep His words because His words are true and right and holy! Thank you, Jesus, for giving me words that last forever and never change. How I praise you because you have come to live in me and make your home in me! Because your love overflows in me, I can love others—not just neighbors, but even enemies! I love you for being so close to me at all times! I thank you that your house is my house and my house is your house!

God Has Prepared Great Things for Me

But as it is written: "Eye has not seen, nor ear heard, nor have entered into the heart of man the things which God has prepared for those who love Him."

1 CORINTHIANS 2:9

Today I can hardly wait to hear what you're telling me! I praise you, Father, that regardless of whether or not I have 20/20 vision, my eyes have not seen, nor are they capable of seeing all the love that you have for me. Thank you that regardless of how good my hearing is my ears will never be able to hear all the wonderful truths you have ready for me. My heart belongs to you, Father, and I'm rejoicing right now because I know you'll have something beautiful beyond words to put in it! Thank you that all these wonderful gifts are especially for me because you love me!

—

God Loves Me No Matter What

But God demonstrates His own love toward us,
in that while we were still sinners, Christ died for us.
ROMANS 5:8

I was the worst of them all, and, yet, you still loved me! Thank you, Father, that you loved me in spite of what I was! You didn't look at my faults and failures, but you looked at what you wanted to see in me! How I praise you, Father, that you let your Son die because your love for me was so great that you were willing to let His blood be shed to save me. I receive your love and enjoy it every day because I remember what that love was willing to do! It thrills me when I realize that I didn't have to clean myself up in order for Jesus to be willing to die for me; He was willing to do it when I was a miserable character!

God Turns Things Around for My Good

However, the L ORD your God would not listen to Balaam but turned the curse into a blessing for you, because the L ORD your God loves you.
DEUTERONOMY 23:5, NIV

Father, how I praise you that you wouldn't allow Balaam to curse Israel because you loved your people so much. You were willing to turn any curse into a blessing each time Balaam opened his mouth. Thank you, Father, that the love which reached your people in the Old Testament times still reaches me today. I love you for that, Father. I thank you that when my mouth gets out of line and begins to say the wrong things that don't glorify you, you can still turn my words around to be a blessing to others! You turn every curse into a blessing in Jesus' name.

I Am Truly Blessed

Whoever has my commandments and keeps them, he it is who loves me. And he who loves me will be loved by my Father, and I will love him and manifest myself to him.
JOHN 14:21, ESV

I praise you, Father, that Jesus has given us commandments to keep, which make the Christian life so simple and straightforward to live. All we have to do is what you tell us to do and refrain from doing the things you tell us not to do. We are blessed and living in your love right now. How we praise you, Jesus, that you have promised to manifest yourself to us because we love you. You've said that you will let yourself be clearly seen and make yourself real to me at all times. I really love you!

God Is Love

He who does not love does not know God,
for God is love.

1 JOHN 4:8

Father, thank you that your Word tells me the greatest commandment is to love you with every fiber of my being, and the second is to love my neighbor as myself. I obey these commandments so that you will live in my heart and fill me up with even more love! I praise you because when you created me, you made me able to receive and to give love, for you are love, and the river of your love flows continually to your people! I rejoice in your love, Father, and I thank you for letting us know, in no uncertain terms, that there is plenty of love for all those who open their hearts to receive it! I love you, Father!

I Will Love Everyone

Dear friends, since God so loved us,
we also ought to love one another.
1 JOHN 4:11, NIV

Thank you, Father, for showing us that you love us so much that there isn't any excuse for us not loving one another! Thank you for giving me a soft heart and the ability to love all my brothers and sisters on this earth. I know I could never do this on my own, but because you love me through all my sin, all my faults, and all my failures, you give me the ability to love even those people who seem unlovable! Thank you, Father, for your Word teaches that everybody deserves love!

I Have a Thankful Heart

*We know how much God loves us, and we have put
our trust in his love. God is love, and all who live in
love live in God, and God lives in them.*

1 JOHN 4:16, NLT

I glorify your name, Father, because I know and
believe how much you love me. You washed my
sin away with the blood of Jesus and there just
isn't any way I can imagine a greater love than that.
There isn't any way I can thank you enough for
what you did. But, Father, I want to try by loving
you with everything I've got and by obeying you in
all things. I thank you, Father, that I dwell in love
because of your love for me. Because of the power of
your love, I live in you and you live in me.

God Gives the Greatest Love

This is My commandment,
that you love one another as I have loved you. Greater
love has no one than this,
than to lay down one's life for his friends.
JOHN 15:12–13

Love is the greatest force in the world, Lord Jesus, and is the most powerful word in the Bible. I thank you for commanding me to love others in the same way that you loved me. Thank you that you not only gave your life for your friends, but you gave it for me, an enemy for many years. How I praise you for showing me the way to love others! I will express your love in me to those I meet, even to those who are hard to love.

I Will Always Love God

"And you shall love the LORD your God with all your heart, with all your soul, with all your mind, and with all your strength." This is the first commandment.

MARK 12:30

Father, I love you with all my mind, my heart, my strength, and my soul! Because you love me so much, it's easy to love you in return. I worship you, Father, because your first commandment concerns love, which is what everyone in the world needs and deserves. Thank you that in loving you, I receive the power to love everyone. I will find a specific individual to love today. I will concentrate on finding a person who needs love, someone who does not have many friends, and whose heart is crying out for love. I'm going to love that person today with your special love.

God Commands Me to Love Everyone

A new command I give you: Love one another.
As I have loved you, so you must love one another.
JOHN 13:34, NIV

Thank you, Father, that Jesus gave me a new commandment. I praise you that people know I am His disciple because I love in a new way. I love others as Jesus loved me! Thank you that Jesus loved me enough to teach me, heal me, and save me from sin by even dying for me! Thank you that this is your limitless love flowing through me right now, a powerful love that enables me to love everyone even as Jesus did. Thank you, Father, that when I obey this commandment to love others, I am at the same time loving you with all my heart, my soul, my mind, and my strength.

I Am Filled
with God's Love

*Then Christ will make his home in your hearts as you
trust in him. Your roots will grow down into God's love
and keep you strong. And may you have the power to
understand, as all God's people should, how wide, how
long, how high, and how deep his love is. May you
experience the love of Christ, though it is too great to
understand fully. Then you will be made complete with
all the fullness of life and power that comes from God.*

EPHESIANS 3:17–19, NLT

Father, I praise you that Jesus lives in me! Jesus,
be more and more at home in my heart! Thank you
that my roots are going all the way down deep into
your soil, which enables me to feel the tremendous
depth of your love for me, even though I know
I will never be able to comprehend it with my
limited mind. Father, I'm so excited because you
promise that some day I will be filled all the way
up to the top with you! Glory!

I Will Love Just as God Loves

And the glory which You gave Me I have given them,
that they may be one just as We are one: I in them,
and You in Me; that they may be made perfect in one,
and that the world may know that You have sent Me,
and have loved them as You have loved Me.

JOHN 17:22–23

Father, I love you so much, for so many different reasons, but especially for the glorious perfect unity I have in Christ Jesus. He lives in me and you live in Him; we're all perfected into one glorious body. Father, how you could ever love me as much as you love Jesus is beyond my human comprehension. I praise you for loving me that much!

I Will Love My Wife Unconditionally

But Ruth said, "Do not urge me to leave you or to return from following you. For where you go I will go, and where you lodge I will lodge. Your people shall be my people, and your God my God. Where you die I will die, and there will I be buried. May the LORD do so to me and more also if anything but death parts me from you."

RUTH 1:16–17, ESV

Thank you, Father, that this verse can also apply to marriage. Thank you for giving my marriage, and every married couple, the most beautiful words to say to each other that can be said. How I thank you, Father, for encouraging me to stay together in marriage. Thank you for the sacredness of human love, as well as divine love, and for allowing me to love my wife in greater ways because of your love pouring through me.

Love Has Made Me Perfect

There is no fear in love; but perfect love casts out fear,
because fear involves torment. But he who fears has not
been made perfect in love.

1 JOHN 4:18

Thank you, Father, that your perfect, complete, full-grown, faultless love turns away every trace of fear. I glory in the knowledge that the devil can't touch me with fear because your love is so complete and surrounds me like a glove. It safely wraps me in a love cocoon. I praise you, Father, for letting me grow into love's complete perfection because of your great love for me. Thank you for a love, which is without a blemish and unparalleled in human understanding, but which is mine because I belong to you. I love you, Father!

I Love God More than Anything

He who loves father or mother more than Me is not worthy of Me. And he who loves son or daughter more than Me is not worthy of Me.

MATTHEW 10:37

Father, I love you more than anything in the whole wide world! I praise you, Father, because you command and demand that I love you more than a mother or father or even my children. Thank you for always knowing what is best for me. By giving you the first place in my life to love you most, you've given me the opportunity to love my own family even more because of your love flowing through me. Thank you for giving me the desire and the ability to love you more than anyone and to cling steadfastly to you and walk in your ways. Thank you, Father, because the love of my family is based on you and not on my own desires. You have first place in my heart!

I Will Walk in Love

*And walk in love, as Christ also has loved us
and given Himself for us, an offering and a sacrifice to
God for a sweet-smelling aroma.*

EPHESIANS 5:2

Father, I'm walking in love! In fact, I'm running in the love of Christ! Thank you! First of all, thank you for loving me so much. Secondly, thank you for letting me share your sacrificial love with others. I'm walking down streets with love, letting it bless people who don't even like me. I'm talking in love to everyone I meet, including those who try to cheat me! I'm thinking in love, even when my thoughts might be trying to go in other directions. I love because you've put love into my heart!

I Am Forgiven and Loved by God

Therefore, I tell you, her many sins have been forgiven—
as her great love has shown. But whoever has been
forgiven little loves little.

LUKE 7:47, NIV

Father, although I was the worst of the sinners, you forgave me so much. It's easy for me to love you wholeheartedly without any reservations whatsoever. I love you, Father, because you didn't just forgive a little, but you forgave everything you might have ever held against me. I love you so very, very much! As a result of your forgiveness, I walk in peace and in freedom from all the problems that are the result of sin! No wonder I love you so much!

I Align with God's Principles

Do not be unequally yoked with unbelievers.
For what partnership has righteousness
with lawlessness? Or what fellowship has light
with darkness?

2 CORINTHIANS 6:14, ESV

Lord, I love you because you tell me exactly how to find favor in your eyes. Thank you for telling me that I'm not to team up with people who don't love you. My inner being tells me that I don't have anything in common with them. Darkness and light don't go together; neither do God and sin. Thank you, Lord, that I walk in the light! Thank you for saving me from mismatched alliances, whether that's in my marriage, in my business, and or in my friendships. There's no way a partnership can work with you on one side and the devil on the other. Thank you for pointing it out to me so vividly to keep me from falling into dangerous places again!

I Will Be Kind and Forgiving

Instead, be kind to each other, tenderhearted, forgiving one another, just as God through Christ has forgiven you.
EPHESIANS 4:32, NLT

Father, thank you for giving me the power to forgive those who have sinned against me, and I praise you for telling me to be kind, tenderhearted, compassionate, and understand-ing because I belong to Christ. I love you, Jesus, for living in and through me, which gives me the power and the desire to forgive each and every person who may have ever hurt me. Father, I praise you because I don't have to keep those little hurts in my memory as a result of your love. Thank you that I can do this quickly, readily, and freely, as it is the way you forgave me.

I Will Serve Others

Let love be without hypocrisy. Abhor what is evil. Cling to what is good. Be kindly affectionate to one another with brotherly love, in honor giving preference to one another; not lagging in diligence, fervent in spirit, serving the Lord.

ROMANS 12:9–11

I hate evil! Father, I love you for putting in my heart such a dislike for the things of the devil and for allowing me to hate that which is wrong. Thank you that I can stand for the good in this world! Father, in this world I can sincerely love others with brotherly affection because of you. I adore you; I hate and loathe everything that is evil or ungodly. I turn in absolute horror from wickedness! I used to love wickedness, and I thank you for delivering me from that love! I prefer others and am diligent, fervent in spirit, serving the Lord!

I Will Love My Neighbor

For the commandments, "You shall not commit adultery, You shall not murder, You shall not steal, You shall not covet," and any other commandment, are summed up in this word: "You shall love your neighbor as yourself."

ROMANS 13:9 ESV

I love you, Father, because you give me the power to live the way you want me to, without wanting to harm or cheat or steal from my neighbors. Thank you, Father. You have wrapped up very neatly all the commandments in this one statement: to love your neighbor as yourself. Thank you, Father. I can love my neighbors because of you.

I Am a Servant of God

For do I now persuade men, or God?
Or do I seek to please men?
For if I still pleased men,
I would not be a servant of Christ.
GALATIANS 1:10

I praise your holy name, Father, because you haven't called me to please people but to please you. Thank you, Father. Now my thoughts can be turned toward you at all times so that I can think about making your heart glad being a servant of Jesus Christ. I thank you for allowing me to serve and follow Jesus! Glory! I don't have to go along with the crowd and do things I don't want to do because I'm afraid of what they might think about me! I'm your willing, happy, and contented servant!

I Will Speak the Truth with Humility

They must not slander anyone and must avoid quarreling. Instead, they should be gentle and show true humility to everyone.

TITUS 3:2, NLT

Father, let the words of my mouth be acceptable in your sight! Let me be filled with so much of your love that my tongue will only have words that are encouraging to other. I will bridle my tongue and let no words that are harmful, hurtful, injurious, malignant, disastrous, or ruinous come out of my mouth. My lips shall speak words of love, bringing strength, hope, and cheer to others. I will not gossip, criticize, complain, or manufacture untruths about anyone. Instead I will keep my conversation full of your love!

I Will Work Well with Others

Then make me truly happy by agreeing wholeheartedly with each other, loving one another, and working together with one mind and purpose.

PHILIPPIANS 2:2

Father, I am filling up with your love so my joy can be complete. I am living in harmony with others and am of the same mind and one in purpose. I will have abundant love for all my brothers and sisters in Christ. I am working toward a unity with people who are different than me so that strife, selfishness, and contentiousness will cease. I will love those whose doctrines do not exactly agree with mine. If they love Jesus and if we are like-minded in that area, we can be in one accord and one mind. Let the little, unimportant things fall by the wayside and let us dwell on the things that last. Thank you for giving me a love that is big enough to encompass doctrinal differences. I'm running over with love! It's splashing on everyone I run into and it blesses everyone it falls on because of your love!

I Will Be Considerate of Others

*Love suffers long and is kind; love does not envy; love
does not parade itself, is not puffed up;
does not behave rudely, does not seek its own,
is not provoked, thinks no evil.*

1 CORINTHIANS 13:4–5

Father, thank you for this love chapter in the
Bible. Thank you for telling me exactly what love
is. Lord, I will not envy, behave rudely, or seek my
own will. Your wonderful love is flowing through
me to reach others. I will not be irritable or touchy.
Thank you, Father, all of this is only possible
because of your love! I praise you that I don't have
to insist on my "rights" and having my own way. I
lost my grudges at the altar of salvation and I will
think no evil of anyone.

I Will Share God's Love with Others

And now abide faith, hope, love, these three;
but the greatest of these is love.
1 CORINTHIANS 13:13

I praise you, Father, for faith, hope, and love. I will abide in each. Thank you that the greatest one of these is love. Without love, it would be difficult to have faith and hope. But with your love, as it is the greatest of all, we also have faith and hope. We have faith in the knowledge that Jesus Christ is coming back and hope that it is going to be soon. We love you because of the joyful and confident expectation of eternal salvation. Thank you that you enable us to have true affection and love for you and for others in this world!

I Am Empowered by God's Love

Now hope does not disappoint, because the love of God has been poured out in our hearts by the Holy Spirit who was given to us.

ROMANS 5:5

Father, I thank you because the love in my human heart is not something I have to try to work up. I can spread your love all over the world because you have poured out this amazing love in my heart by the Holy Spirit. Your love is a beautiful gift you give to your children. Thank you, Father, that the world can see your love in me. I don't have to have unbelief or distrust, which would cause me to waver about whether or not I could really love someone. Instead, I am empowered by my faith in you and your promises!

I Am More than a Conqueror

But in all these things we overwhelmingly conquer through Him who loved us.
ROMANS 8:37, NASB

Glory to God, I'm more than a conqueror! Father, how I praise you for that word *all*! Thank you for letting me know that I win *all* the battles because of your love. The same love that allowed Jesus Christ to die on a cross for me makes me more than a conqueror in *all* areas of my life. I don't have to bow to the devil in any area because you've said in *all* these things I am more than a conqueror through Him who loved me. Thank you, Father, for another month of victory in Jesus! Thank you that I always have a surpassing victory in everything because of your great love!

JULY

Freedom from Fear

As you make these declarations, we believe that you will be delivered from the bondage of fear and be totally and completely liberated by declaring God's powerful Word. May the Holy Spirit fill you with His perfect and eternal love, which casts out all fear.

I Am Strong and Courageous

And David said to his son Solomon, "Be strong and of good courage, and do it; do not fear nor be dismayed, for the LORD God—my God—will be with you. He will not leave you nor forsake you, until you have finished all the work for the service of the house of the LORD."

1 CHRONICLES 28:20

Today I'm strong, courageous, and afraid of nothing. Thank you, Father, because you care about every little detail of my life. I am not frightened by the task. You always are with me. I praise you, Father, that you are with me as I finish the work you have given me to do. Thank you that I don't have to live the Christian life in my own strength, but instead, I can rest in you who strengthens me!

I Am as Bold as a Lion

The wicked flee when no one pursues,
but the righteous are bold as a lion.
PROVERBS 28:1

Today I am bold, bold, *bold!* Father, I praise you
for giving me the boldness of a lion! Thank you for
the righteousness that comes from you. I act and
make decisions with the courage that comes from
knowing you are with me in all I do. The wicked flee
because they're afraid that what they've done will
catch up with them and destroy them. I'm always on
the winning side! I can go into any situation of the
devil's making, and the wicked will flee before me
because you've made me bold as a lion!

—

I Have a Sound Mind

For God has not given us a spirit of fear,
but of power and of love and of a sound mind.

2 TIMOTHY 1:7

I have a sound mind at all times because I have the mind of Christ! I love you, praise you, and thank you, Father because you haven't given me a spirit of fear. I rejoice because fear is never from you. Because you have given me power over the devil and all his doings, I can boldly dismiss any thoughts or feelings of fear that come before me. Thank you, Father, that you've given me a sound mind and the power to face any situation and be victorious in it!

My Life Is Abundant

The thief does not come except to steal, and to kill,
and to destroy. I have come that they may have life,
and that they may have it more abundantly.
JOHN 10:10

Father, I praise you for the day you granted
freedom to this nation. But more than that, I thank
you for the freedom and abundance of life you
have granted me through your Son, Jesus Christ,
who came to defeat the devil and all his evil and
destructive ways. Jesus came to free me from the
bondage of the devil's fear so that the devil can
never again steal the blessings of life from me or
my children. Jesus is the way, the truth, and the
life, and through Him I have the abundant life you
want all your children to have!

I Have Authority and Power

Behold, I give you the authority to trample on serpent and scorpion, and over all the power of the enemy, and nothing shall by any means hurt you.

LUKE 10:19

Father, you have given me the power to tread on all the works of the devil without harm coming to me! I rejoice that you've turned the tables on the devil. Now I have power over all the power of the enemy, and he has to run from me! I praise you for making me immune to the poison of the enemy. I am triumphant in times of trouble and at peace in the midst of strife. Thank you, Father, for making me a spiritual warrior so I can stomp on the works of the enemy wherever I find them!

—

I Commit My Plans to God

*Commit to the LORD whatever you do,
and he will establish your plans.*
PROVERBS 16:3, NIV

Father, I place all my cares, worries, and defeats on the alter! I commit them to you and trust that you will take care of them completely. I'm not going to worry about them any more! I thank you that all my thoughts are becoming agreeable to your will, and I will not reflect on what will be unsatisfactory to you. I turn my back on all the lusts of the flesh and roll my works upon you. I hear your voice and do only the works you tell me to do. I'm excited because I now have complete assurance that everything I do is going to be established and succeed. How I praise you that you make no plans for failure in your Word!

God Provides for My Needs

The Lord is my shepherd; I shall not want.
He makes me to lie down in green pastures;
He leads me beside the still waters.
PSALM 23:1-2

I love and praise you, Father, because in the abiding love and care you pour upon me, I fear no evil. With you as my shepherd, I'm surrounded by your protective power at all times. I rejoice that I can relax and enjoy your green pastures and still waters. Wherever you lead me, I have complete trust that all my needs are met. I thank you, Father, for seeing to it that I lack nothing. I praise you because I can look to you for everything I need in my life without worry because you always provide for me. Thank you, Father.

—

I Have Courage

Be strong and of good courage,
do not fear nor be afraid of them;
for the LORD your God,
He is the One who goes with you.
He will not leave you nor forsake you.

DEUTERONOMY 31:6

Father, I'm strong! I'm courageous! I praise you because I'm not afraid. You are with me in all your power and glory and righteousness, and nothing can withstand your might! I give thanks that you are the Lord my God who never fails me or leaves me no matter what kind of difficulty or challenge I have to face. You are the strength in my soul and the courage in my heart and I fear nothing. Hallelujah! I'm blessed with victory!

—

I Have No Fear

*The LORD is my light and my salvation; Whom shall
I fear? The LORD is the strength of my life; Of whom
shall I be afraid? When the wicked came against me
to eat up my flesh, my enemies and foes, they stumbled
and fell. Though an army may encamp against me, my
heart shall not fear; Though war may rise against me,
in this I will be confident.*

PSALM 27:1–3

Thank you, Father, for shining your light on
the path of righteousness so I can see to walk in
your ways. I will not fear anyone or anything! You
are my strength and my shield. I fear neither the
wickedness of my enemies nor the tricks of the
devil because you will cause them to stumble and
fall. In the midst of the battle I will be confident in
you and your love for me. Hallelujah!

God Hides Me in Safety

For in the time of trouble He shall hide me in His pavilion; in the secret place of His tabernacle He shall hide me; He shall set me high upon a rock.

PSALM 27:5

I rejoice, Father, that you protect and hide me from any kind of trouble that comes my way! Thank you that you always hide me in your pavilion or in the secret of your tabernacle where the wicked dare not follow. How I bless and praise you, Father. No matter what deceitful schemes the devil comes up with to disrupt my life, you take me out of harm's way and set me upon a rock where the enemy can't touch me! I love you, Father!

I Sing Praises to God

And now my head shall be lifted up above my enemies all around me; Therefore I will offer sacrifices of joy in His tabernacle; I will sing, yes, I will sing praises to the LORD.

PSALM 27:6

Father, I praise you because I don't have to look up at my enemies. You lift my head above them so that I'm seeing from your perspective! You are the God of deliverance and the God of my salvation. I offer sacrifices of joy to you in celebration of the wonderful way you take care of me! I'm singing praises to you because you lift me above the trials and tribulations of the world. I love you with all my heart!

I am Free from Sin and Death

There is therefore now no condemnation for those who are in Christ Jesus. For the law of the Spirit of life has set you free in Christ Jesus from the law of sin and death.
ROMANS 8:1-2, ESV

How I praise you, Father, that there is no condemnation or fear in my life. I rejoice because I am in Jesus Christ and I walk after the Spirit! Thank you for the promises in your Word that say that all my sins are forgiven. You don't even remember them, so I don't have any fear of the past. I praise you, Father, that by the law of the Spirit of life in Jesus, I'm free from the law of sin and death. So everything before me and everything in my future is blessed! Hallelujah!

God Is Always with Me

This is my command—
be strong and courageous!
Do not be afraid or discouraged.
For the Lord your God
is with you wherever you go.
JOSHUA 1:9, NLT

How I thank you, Father, the power and truth of your commandment make me strong and fill me with courage! Fear and dismay have no part in my life because my strength is in you, and I trust you in all things. When the devil comes against me, I am brave and jubilant for I know you are with me every moment day and night, and I have victory over all the power of darkness! Thank you, Father, that you are with me wherever I go!

I Drink from God's Well of Salvation

"Behold, God is my salvation, I will trust and not be afraid; For the LORD GOD is my strength and song, And He has become my salvation." Therefore you will joyously draw water from the springs of salvation.

ISAIAH 12:2–3, NASB

Father, I rejoice that you are my salvation! Because of this, I place my whole trust in you and I am never afraid or anxious in anything. I rejoice in you because you are my strength and my song, and with so much confidence and happiness bubbling through me, I sing your praises everywhere I go. Father, I thank you for the wells of your salvation. Your living water renews, blesses, and refreshes my life, giving me such joy that I feel like telling everyone I meet what a glorious God you are!

The Power of Death Is Broken

Inasmuch then as the children have partaken of flesh and blood, He Himself likewise shared in the same, that through death He might destroy him who had the power of death, that is, the devil, and release those who through fear of death were all their lifetime subject to bondage.

HEBREWS 2:14–15

Thank you, Jesus, for taking death upon yourself to destroy the one who had the power of death. Thank you because I'm free of the fear of death and the desperate hunger for power, money, and the things of this world that come from fearing death. I praise you, Father, that Jesus delivered me from sin, the devil, and bondage to fear by shedding His blood for me upon the cross. I thank you for that glorious promise of eternal life in your kingdom! Because death couldn't hold Jesus in the grave, it won't hold me either. I'm rejoicing because my eternal home is with you! Thank you, Father, for the priceless blessing of eternal life!

I Am Made Perfect in Love

There is no fear in love; but perfect love casts out fear,
because fear involves torment. But he who fears has not
been made perfect in love.
1 JOHN 4:18

I praise and thank you, glorious Father. Your
perfect love flows through me in such great measure
that it has cast out fear of any kind and all kinds!
I thank you, Father, for removing the torment of
fear from my life, for torment comes from the devil,
and he has to run from the power of your perfect
love! I'm blessed beyond my wildest dreams, Father,
because I'm being perfected in your wonderful love!

God Is My Ultimate Refuge

God is our refuge and strength, a very present help in trouble. Therefore we will not fear, though the earth be removed, and though the mountains be carried into the midst of the sea; though its waters roar and be troubled, though the mountains shake with its swelling. Selah.

PSALM 46:1–3

Father, I thank and praise you because you are my refuge and strength. You are my help at the moment trouble comes. You are the God of my salvation and you will take care of me no matter what happens. Father, I praise you because you are the Creator, the God of everything, and for that reason, I don't fear anything. Whether the world falls apart or a great earthquake rocks the mountains, I'll be saved and protected by your loving power! Hallelujah!

I Walk in the Light of God

In God, whose word I praise, in the LORD, whose word I praise—in God I trust and am not afraid. What can man do to me? I am under vows to you, my God; I will present my thank offerings to you. For you have delivered me from death and my feet from stumbling, that I may walk before God in the light of life.

PSALM 56:10–13, NIV

Father, I trust you so much that there's no room in my life for fear! I love your promises for you always keep them, and I thank you for all the help you've given me. I thank you for saving me from death and for keeping my feet from slipping so I can walk in your ways. Father, I rejoice in your light!

God Is My Refuge

He who dwells in the shelter of the Most High will abide in the shadow of the Almighty. I will say to the LORD, "My refuge and my fortress, my God, in whom I trust."

PSALM 91:1-2

I thank you, Father, because I abide in the safety and comfort of your shadow where no evil can touch me. You are my refuge and my fortress, and I thank you and praise you that you are a God who keeps all His promises to His children. My trust is always fulfilled in you. Because I dwell in the secret place of the highest, the devil can't make fear fall upon me. Instead, I am lifted up and blessed over and over by the love and power with which you surround me!

Angels Watch Over Me

No evil shall befall you, nor shall any plague come
near your dwelling; for He shall give His angels charge
over you, to keep you in all your ways.
PSALM 91:10-11

Father, thank you that no evil can befall me, and
no plague or sickness can come near my house
because you said so! Thank you that I don't have
to worry about these things any more. You send
your angels and charge them to take care of me in
every way! I praise you, Father, for loving me so
much that your angels stick by me night and day to
guard and protect me, my house, and family from
everything the devil might try to do to us. Thank
you, Father, that your Word frees me from fear of
sickness, calamity, and disease! Hallelujah!

I Win by the Spirit of God

Then he said to me, "This is the word of the LORD to
Zerubbabel: Not by might, nor by power, but by my
Spirit, says the LORD of hosts."

ZECHARIAH 4:6

Thank you, Father, that I don't have to have fear.
You've promised that I don't have to win battles in
my own strength or power, but instead, you will
win them for me by your Spirit! Glory to the Lord
of hosts! Here I am, winning again!

I Trust in God

Whoever gives heed to instruction prospers,
and blessed is the one who trusts in the LORD.
PROVERBS 16:20, NIV

I love to receive your blessings, Father, because I know that everything that comes from you is good! I obey you without hesitation because everything you tell me to do comes from your righteousness, and I rejoice in your righteousness. I have no fear, nervousness, worry, or care about the future or about problems because your blessings are upon me. I'm happy and I'm singing your praises because I put my trust, my faith, my confidence, and my hope in you. I'm full of anticipation for the good things in life, and fear went out the window when faith and trust came in!

I Sleep Peacefully

The LORD by wisdom founded the earth, by understanding He established the heavens. By His knowledge the deeps were broken up and the skies drip with dew. My son, let them not vanish from your sight; Keep sound wisdom and discretion, so they will be life to your soul and adornment to your neck. Then you will walk in your way securely and your foot will not stumble. When you lie down, you will not be afraid; When you lie down, your sleep will be sweet. Do not be afraid of sudden fear nor of the onslaught of the wicked when it comes; For the LORD will be your confidence and will keep your foot from being caught.

PROVERBS 3:19–26, NASB

Father, your wisdom that founded the earth is the same wisdom that guides my life and guards me from fear of falling or stumbling. You are my confidence and by your wisdom and knowledge there is life in my soul and grace in my life. Father, I am awed by the magnificent miracle of your creation, and my sleep is sweet because I am protected day and night by your mighty power! Hallelujah!

God Is Always Faithful

The fear of man brings a snare,
but whoever trusts in the LORD shall be safe.
PROVERBS 29:25

I thank you, Father, for taking all fear from me. Fear is just an invitation for the devil to take advantage with one of his deceitful snares. I love and praise you, Father, for being the God I can trust with all my heart. I do trust you because you are always faithful to keep your children safe and filled with blessings. You are wonderful to me!

God Fights My Battles

And Moses said to the people, "Do not be afraid. Stand still, and see the salvation of the Lord, which He will accomplish for you today. For the Egyptians whom you see today, you shall see again no more forever. The Lord will fight for you, and you shall hold your peace." And the Lord said to Moses, "Why do you cry to Me? Tell the children of Israel to go forward."

EXODUS 14:13–15

Father, thank you for the simple, direct, and powerful ways you deliver us from seemingly hopeless situations. No situation is hopeless before your mighty power. I move forward in Jesus' name through every difficulty. You are fighting for me and I will be at peace. You are a God of wonderful miracles and faithfulness to your people!

I Will Not Fear

Don't be afraid, for I am with you. Don't be discouraged, for I am your God. I will strengthen you and help you. I will hold you up with my victorious right hand. See, all your angry enemies lie there, confused and humiliated. Anyone who opposes you will die and come to nothing. You will look in vain for those who tried to conquer you. Those who attack you will come to nothing. For I hold you by your right hand—I, the LORD your God. And I say to you, "Don't be afraid. I am here to help you. Though you are a lowly worm, O Jacob, don't be afraid, people of Israel, for I will help you. I am the LORD, your Redeemer. I am the Holy One of Israel."

ISAIAH 41:10-14, NLT

I am thankful, Father, that you bring your people to victory no matter what the situation. Your right hand is more powerful than all the armies of the world with all their weapons, and no one can stand against me because you are for me! Thank you, Father, that I am victorious in all situations!

God Calls Me by My Name

But now, thus says the LORD, who created you,
O Jacob, and He who formed you, O Israel:
"Fear not, for I have redeemed you; I have called you by
your name; You are Mine. When you pass through the
waters, I will be with you; And through the rivers, they
shall not overflow you. When you walk through the fire,
you shall not be burned, nor shall the flame scorch you.

ISAIAH 43:1–2

How I praise you, Father, for redeeming me, calling me by name, rescuing me from trouble, difficulty, and oppression, and saving me! Glorious Father, I rejoice that you openly declare in your Word that I am yours! Wherever I go—East, West, North or South —you call me to yourself because you love me. Because you are with me, I don't fear deep water, fire, or all the power of the devil for you will rescue me from all of them! Father, I praise you and thank you for who you are!

I Will Not Be Afraid

Do not be afraid of those who kill the body but cannot kill the soul. Rather, be afraid of the One who can destroy both soul and body in hell. Are not two sparrows sold for a penny? Yet not one of them will fall to the ground outside your Father's care. And even the very hairs of your head are all numbered. So don't be afraid; you are worth more than many sparrows.

MATTHEW 10:28–31, NIV

How exciting, Father, to know that you love me so much you have even numbered the hairs on my head! Not only do you know those I have, you know those I have lost. I don't fear any person on this earth because you notice when the smallest bird falls to the ground. You always know when I need your help, and instantly, you are right there with me. I praise you, Father, for getting rid of all my worries because you love me so much! I'm certainly glad to be worth more to you than a sparrow!

I Rest in God's Arms

The eternal God is your refuge, and underneath are the everlasting arms; He will thrust out the enemy from before you, and will say, "Destroy!"

DEUTERONOMY 33:27

Father, I give praise to you for being the eternal God who has complete power over all things past, present, and future. I thank you for forgiving all my sins of the past, loving me right now, and giving me a wonderful future to look forward to! I praise you for holding me with love in your everlasting arms. You are my refuge, and nothing can harm me regardless of the situation. Thank you for always going before me in your glory and power so that the wicked are thrust out of my path. Father, I love your everlasting arms!

God Lights My Path

What you decide on will be done,
and light will shine on your ways.
JOB 22:28, NIV

Bless you, Father, that I don't have to worry about whether or not I'm going to be a failure or a success. Your blueprint for my life makes it so simple. I'm throwing fear out the window because you've said that what I decide on will be done. How I praise you. I'm walking in the light of your favor, and it's shining upon my ways! Father, what a privilege to be able to follow your Word so easily and know that you make us winner all the time. I love you for that!

My Heart Is Thankful

Do not be anxious about anything, but in every situation, by prayer and petition, with thanksgiving, present your requests to God. And the peace of God, which transcends all understanding, will guard your hearts and your minds in Christ Jesus.
PHILIPPIANS 4:6–7, NIV

How I thank and praise you, Father, because I don't need to worry about anything. Your love for me is so great that I am filled with and surrounded by your mighty power at all times. Because of your promises and your Word, I have peace in all circumstances. Your peace surpasses all understanding. It is a peace that guards my heart and mind in Christ Jesus. I praise you for the wonderful blessing of that peace! Hallelujah!

AUGUST

Strength

August is the time when energy can start to drag because of the long, hot, summer days. Thank God for His Word that declares: *"But those who wait on the Lord shall renew their strength; They shall mount up with wings like eagles, they shall run and not be weary, they shall walk and not faint"* (Isaiah 40:31).

Let's mount up with wings as eagles and soar higher this month than we ever have. Declare these Scriptures four and five times every day!

Whether these Scriptures are new or familiar, remind yourself of what God has for you in order to make you stronger in your daily life.

Why not select at least two Scripture verses this month to memorize? Say them out loud or in your thoughts every day, as often as they come to your mind.

I Listen to the Words of God

Jesus answered, "It is written:
'Man shall not live on bread alone,
but on every word that comes
from the mouth of God.'"
MATTHEW 4:4

Father, I thank you because I don't have to exist only on earthly food. I live in an eternal realm and my most delicious meals and desserts are the words that come out of your mouth! Thank you, Father, that your Word is true, and everything you have said will come to pass because you spoke it. You are a God who cannot lie. Thank you that I don't have to depend just on meat and potatoes for strength, but I can depend on you from whom our real strength comes! Thank you for saying, "It is written," because the devil has to run when I say those words to him!

I Will Overcome

And they overcame him by the blood of the Lamb
and by the word of their testimony,
and they did not love their lives to the death.

REVELATION 12:11

Thank you, Father, because the blood of the Lamb overcomes all things and makes us overcomers! I praise you, Father, because the blood of Jesus was shed for each and every one of us, and this blood is more powerful than the devil. He trembles when he comes close to the bloodline that surrounds us! The very word of my testimony gives me power over all of the enemy! Thank you, Father, that when I speak your Word, it becomes my word, and is power!

I Share God's Good News

*The Spirit of the Lord is upon me, because he has
anointed me to proclaim good news to the poor.
He has sent me to proclaim liberty to the captives and
recovering of sight to the blind,
to set at liberty those who are oppressed.*
LUKE 4:18, ESV

Father, how I bless you that because I'm a joint
heir with Jesus, this promise is mine. The Spirit of
the Lord is upon me and I know what I am to do.
I share the good news, love the brokenhearted who
feel that nobody loves them. I speak your words of
deliverance to those who are captive and slaves to
habits of the flesh. I praise you that your anointing
is here at all times whether I feel it or not. Thank
you for giving me such a privilege!

I Value Nobility and Truth

Finally, brethren, whatever things are true, whatever things are noble, whatever things are just, whatever things are pure, whatever things are lovely, whatever things are of good report, if there is any virtue and if there is anything praiseworthy—meditate on these things.

PHILIPPIANS 4:8

Father, I praise you because I don't have to think on the evil things of the devil. I don't have to worry about the problems of the world and the crises that arise. I don't have to be disturbed or tormented because I follow your instructions and think on uplifting things, which are true, honest, just, pure, and lovely. I meditate upon all that is good, virtuous, and praiseworthy. I fix my eyes on you and these things, Father.

I Carry God's Weapon of Truth

We use God's mighty weapons, not worldly weapons, to knock down the strongholds of human reasoning and to destroy false arguments. We destroy every proud obstacle that keeps people from knowing God. We capture their rebellious thoughts and teach them to obey Christ.

2 CORINTHIANS 10:4–5, NLT

Thank you, Father, that my weapons are not of this world. They are spiritual and powerful because they come from you. You do not expect me to use carnal weapons; you give me the mighty sword of your Spirit, which is the Word of God. I cast down my vain imaginations, which the devil would like to put into my mind. I bring all of my thoughts to the wonderful obedience of Christ because of your mighty power! All rebellious thoughts will obey Christ and my mind will be fixed upon Him.

My Words Edify Others

Do not let any unwholesome talk come out of your mouths, but only what is helpful for building others up according to their needs, that it may benefit those who listen.

EPHESIANS 4:29, NIV

Father, how I praise you for instructing what should come out of my mouth. Thank you for telling me that I shouldn't mock, ridicule, deny truth, confuse, or speak corruption in any way. Words that don't edify and minister grace to others do not glorify you. I will not complain, criticize, or use unwholesome and worthless talk. I praise you that every word will be used to glorify you at all times so that it may benefit all who listen.

God Renews My Strength

They who wait for the LORD shall renew their strength; they shall mount up with wings like eagles; they shall run and not be weary; they shall walk and not faint.

ISAIAH 40:31, ESV

Today I feel like flying! I rejoice and thank you, Father, for the supernatural power and energy you give me. When I serve and wait upon you, I can mount up like an eagle and draw close to you, as the eagles draw close to the sun. When I run, I'm not weary, and when I walk, I don't faint. Even when I'm tired, you give me the extra boost of energy, strength, and vigor I need. When my enthusiasm begins to lag and my zeal begins to fade, you're right there with those heavenly supplements. I'm running with no weariness and walking strong and upright!

God Gives Me Divine Rest

Come to Me, all you who labor and are heavy laden, and I will give you rest. Take My yoke upon you and learn from Me, for I am gentle and lowly in heart, and you will find rest for your souls.

MATTHEW 11:28–29

I'm so rested, Father. Thank you for the privilege of knowing that when I am faced with problems, I can come to Jesus and He will give me rest. Thank you, Father, that your burden is light, and when I take your yoke upon me, I have joyful rest in you. I praise you because you are always gentle and there to take my burdens from me. How I praise you that your yoke is wholesome and good and not harsh, hard, sharp, or pressing. Instead, it remains comfortable, gracious, and pleasant! Bless you for that divine rest!

God Answers My Call

Call to Me, and I will answer you, and show you great and mighty things, which you do not know.
JEREMIAH 33:3

I want to see more and more! I love you, Father, for always answering me when I call! Thank you that in answer to my call you will show me great and mighty things, which I don't even know about! You show me the supernatural and new understanding about who you are each day. I'm calling and will continue to call because I want to see your glory and your power more than I ever have before. I delight in and want you to show me things beyond my wildest dreams or imagination.

I Will See God's Glory

*But truly, as I live, all the earth shall be filled
with the glory of the LORD.*
NUMBERS 14:21

Father, I want to see your glory! I want to bask in
the magnificence of your presence, and I can hardly
wait to see the entire earth filled with your glory! I
want to see the whole earth filled with your saints
who are full of glory and joy. Great is the glory of
the Lord. I thank you that you are a sun and shield,
and you give grace and glory! Father, you are a
shield for me, my glory, and the lifter of my head!
I bless you that even though darkness covers the
earth, your glory shall be seen on us!

I Will Sing and Rejoice with Joy

So the ransomed of the LORD shall return, and come to Zion with singing, with everlasting joy on their heads. They shall obtain joy and gladness; sorrow and sighing shall flee away.

ISAIAH 51:11

I'm redeemed by the blood of the Lamb! I thank you that I can sing all the time because your everlasting joy is always pouring upon my head. I thank you that this is an everlasting joy that will never fade away. How I praise you. You don't give me sorrow and sadness, but instead, you give me joy, joy, *joy!* I love you because sorrow and mourning are fleeing away from my life, just as you have promised. How I love you and praise you for all the promises that are mine!

My Steps are Ordered by God

The steps of a man are established by the LORD, when he delights in his way.

PSALM 37:23, ESV

Father, I rejoice that I'm walking in the steps you have ordered. Thank you that you direct each and every step I take. I don't have to worry about the direction I'm going. I'm walking exactly where you tell me to walk. I rejoice because the way you direct my steps is sure and true, superior to anything I could do to find my own way. I'm delighted because it doesn't make any difference if I'm going east, west, north or south. You keep my footsteps going in the right direction. I praise you because you aren't only interested in my entire trip, but you're interested in every single step I take!

I Can Prophesy

Do not neglect the gift that is in you, which was given to you by prophecy with the laying on of the hands of the eldership. Meditate on these things; give yourself entirely to them, that your progress may be evident to all.

1 TIMOTHY 4:14–15

Father, I praise you because the Holy Spirit gave me that special, inward gift. I am practicing, cultivating, and meditating on all these things so that your grace may be evident to all. I am not going to neglect the helps you have given me to live the Christian life or to minister in the life of someone else, but I am stirring them up. I give myself entirely to you and the gifts that you've placed within me. I am a blessing to all.

God Makes
My Way Perfect

God is my strength and power,
and He makes my way perfect.

2 SAMUEL 22:33

Father, how I praise you that you are my strength and my power. I am not satisfied with the things of this world and my own strength because you have given me your very own strength and power. Father, thank you for being willing to make my way perfect. The energy I have comes from the mighty energy that Jesus Christ puts in me, energizing and empowering me to do what He wants me to do. Thank you that you are my strong fortress and because you guide me, you set me free! Thank you, Father!

God Strengthens Me

He gives power to the weak,
and to those who have no might
He increases strength.

ISAIAH 40:29

Father, I love you even during my weaknesses and
faults. I will not rely on my own abilities, so I put
my whole trust in you! Thank you for the power
that you give to me when I'm weak and faint. When
I'm worn out and undone, you cause me to not
look to myself and my solutions. You increase my
strength, causing it to multiply and abound. Even
in my darkest moments, you continually charge and
recharge my spiritual batteries with supernatural
strength! I worship you for this, Father!

I Am Loaded with God's Benefits

Blessed be the Lord, who daily loads us with benefits, the God of our salvation!

PSALM 68:19

I praise you, love you, and worship you, Father, for giving me so many benefits day after day. Your blessings are not a one-time thing, but instead, you daily load me down with all your wonderful benefits, promises, and blessings. You are a river to me! I bless you, the God of my salvation! As I look over this day, Father, I praise you because you don't just give me a little sampling of benefits. I'm excited that you have an overabundance of everything. You load me and continue to load me with your blessings and benefits!

I Have Perfect Peace

You will keep him in perfect peace,
whose mind is stayed on You,
because he trusts in You.
ISAIAH 26:3

How I love and adore you, Father, because my heart, my mind, and my soul have perfect and constant peace. Your Word says that if I keep my mind on you and trust, peace is mine. Jesus, you are the Prince of Peace and I fix my eyes upon you. I don't lean on my own understanding. Instead I lean on your trustworthy ways and I hope in you. Thank you that my mind can confidently and continually stay on you!

Heaven Is Waiting for Me

Do not let your hearts be troubled. You believe in God; believe also in me. My Father's house has many rooms; if that were not so, would I have told you that I am going there to prepare a place for you? And if I go and prepare a place for you, I will come back and take you to be with me that you also may be where I am.

JOHN 14:1–3, NIV

Thank you, Jesus, for giving me an untroubled heart. I believe in you and your great love for me. You are preparing a place for me where you are. I am excited to think about what you are building. It is magnificent and far beyond what I can imagine. I look forward to your return so that I can be with you forever. Thank you, Jesus, for giving me such an exciting future!

God Leads My Path

I will bring the blind by a way they did not know;
I will lead them in paths they have not known.
I will make darkness light before them, and crooked
places straight. These things I will do for them,
and not forsake them.

ISAIAH 42:16

Once I was blind, but now I see. Even before you saved me, you directed my footsteps so that I would go down paths to lead me to you. I praise you that my steps are ordered by the Lord, and you turn the darkness inside out and make it light. You take the most crooked path imaginable and straighten it out. You are doing this for me because you love me. Father, I praise you for your total protection at all times.

God's Law Is in My Heart

"This is the covenant that I will make with them after those days," says the LORD: "I will put My laws into their hearts, and in their minds I will write them," then He adds, *"Their sins and their lawless deeds I will remember no more."*

HEBREWS 10:16–17

Father, how I praise you. Your offering of your perfect Lamb has completely cleansed me! I love you for putting your laws right into my heart and writing them into my mind. I don't depend only on memorizing words from the law because your Holy Spirit reminds me of them constantly. Father, I love you for forgiving and forgetting all my sins and iniquities. I praise you that I don't have to remember them either because you have forgotten them!

God Hears Me

The righteous cry out, and the LORD hears,
and delivers them out of all their troubles.

PSALM 34:17

Lord, I see that you are so very good. When I cry out for help, you are there to deliver me at all times. I magnify the Lord, and I exalt your holy name. You always hear me. You have no hearing problems and your ears are tuned to the righteous at all times. Even though many evils confront me, you deliver me out of all of them. You redeem the life of your servants, and none who take refuge in you shall be condemned or held guilty! Thank you for being my deliverer!

The Spirit of God Is with Me

*"As for me, this is my covenant with them," says the L*ORD*. "My Spirit, who is on you, will not depart from you, and my words that I have put in your mouth will always be on your lips, on the lips of your children and on the lips of their descendants—from this time on and forever," says the L*ORD*.*

ISAIAH 59:21, NIV

Father, I thank you for the covenant you gave to me. I thank you for the words that you have put in my mouth. I praise you that your words shall not depart out of my mouth, nor out of the mouths of my children, nor out of the mouths of my grandchildren. Thank you, Father, for not only blessing me personally, but also for blessing me down through all generations that follow me. I praise you that their hearts will be so in tune with you that their mouths will be pure and speak your words at all times. I love you, Father, for this wonderful promise.

I Will Arise

Arise, shine; for your light has come!
And the glory of the LORD is risen upon you.
ISAIAH 60:1

Father, thank you for Jesus, the light of the world, who lives in me. I praise you because I don't have to lie down and wallow in misery, but I arise from the depression and discouragement in which circumstances have kept me. You constantly let your light shine through me. I thank you that I have risen to a new life, and I am radiant with the glory of the Lord. Your glory is risen upon me! I can't see it, but I praise you that the world can— just because you said so!

My Joy Is Full

These things I have spoken to you,
that My joy may remain in you,
and that your joy may be full.
JOHN 15:11

Father, how I praise you for your words. They are words of hope, inspiration, assurance, and security for all the problems of life. Those words have I hidden in my heart so I might not sin against you. When I keep them safely tucked away in there to be a constant reminder to me of your love and perfection at all times, my joy remains, and my cup of joy is full, complete, and overflowing. I thank you for this. My *joy* is full! It isn't half full. It isn't a quarter full; it's full all the way up to the top because your Word says so!

I Am Made New

*So then, brethren, we are under obligation,
not to the flesh, to live according to the flesh.*
ROMANS 8:12, NASB

How I praise you, Father, that I have absolutely
no obligation to my old nature! I don't ever have
to do what it tempts me to, and even when my old
nature begs me to do something, I don't have to
obey it because there are absolutely no obligations
left. I am no longer a debtor to my old nature, so I
do not have to live a life ruled by the standard set
up by the dictates of the flesh. I praise you, Father,
because the old way was death, but the new way is
life! Hallelujah!

I Am Co-Heir with Christ

Now if we are children, then we are heirs—
heirs of God and co-heirs with Christ,
if indeed we share in his sufferings
in order that we may also share in his glory.
ROMANS 8:17, NIV

Father, I praise you because I am your child.
I am an heir of God and a co-heir with Christ.
Thank you because I share your treasures and
have everything that you gave to Jesus! Hallelujah!
You are so good to me and I love being your
child. I am blessed to share in your sufferings and
in your glory. This is one of the greatest of all
treasures—your abiding, everlasting, continuing,
overwhelming, glorious love!

God Is Sovereign

One God and Father of all, who is above all,
and through all, and in you all.
EPHESIANS 4:6

Father, how I love you because I don't have to worry about which God to serve. You are the only true God, the Father of us all, and you are sovereign above all. I don't have to worry about whose God is best. You're living and flowing in every part of me: my eyes, nose, mouth, ears, arms, hands, fingers, legs, feet, and even my toes. You are filling all of me afresh with your Spirit right now, and I thank you, Father.

My Trust Is in God

In you, O Lord, I put my trust;
let me never be put to shame.

PSALM 71:1

Praise you, Father; my trust is in you. When problems arise and pressures come, I will not be perplexed because I know you and my trust is in you, in whom there is all wisdom and truth. I thank you, Father, that I don't have to search around and try to find someone whom I can trust, but I am secure in the knowledge of confidently taking refuge in you at all times! I will not be put the shame because I place my trust in you.

I Will Hold Fast to God's Words

Do all things without complaining and disputing, that you may become blameless and harmless, children of God without fault in the midst of a crooked and perverse generation, among whom you shine as lights in the world, holding fast the word of life, so that I may rejoice in the day of Christ that I have not run in vain or labored in vain.

PHILIPPIANS 2:14–16

Thank you, Father. I don't have to argue and complain because you've given me a power that keeps me above all of the things of the flesh. Thank you for your instructions on how I can live a clean and innocent life. Father, I thank you that I am a light beaming your love all over the world as I hold out to all people your Word of life. I hold fast to you and will rejoice in the day of Christ because I have run my race well. I look forward to hearing you say, "Well done!"

God Does Not Waver

He did not waver at the promise of God through unbelief, but was strengthened in faith, giving glory to God, and being fully convinced that what He had promised He was also able to perform.

ROMANS 4:20–21

Father, I praise you that I don't have to waver with doubt at any of your promises. Your promises are exceedingly true and will come to pass. You are strengthening me in faith and I give glory to you. I praise you that your Word is full of promises for me and you will accomplish each and every one of them. I love you, Father, for being a God with whom all things are possible.

Sin Has No Power over Me

We know that our old sinful selves were crucified with Christ so that sin might lose its power in our lives. We are no longer slaves to sin. For when we died with Christ we were set free from the power of sin.

ROMANS 6:6–7, NLT

Father, I praise you that I can go to my own spiritual funeral and see myself dead to sin! I praise you that in our dying to self you have totally and completely removed me from sin. I praise you for the end of self. I love you, Father, for giving me another month of victory and joy. I am no longer a slave and I don't ever have to live in the flesh again! You have set me free from the power of sin. Hallelujah!

SEPTEMBER

Healing

Did you know that salvation not only includes the forgiveness of our sins, but also the healing of our bodies? Even if we don't get healed right away, healing is still *for* us. God does not want us sick!

We can call upon the name of Jesus for healing. The name of Jesus is above every disease!

God has given us another avenue for healing. Mark 16:18 says, *"They will lay hands on the sick, and they will recover."* We can go to a Spirit-filled believer, have them lay hands on us, and receive the healing we need.

Jesus said to us, *"Behold, I give you the authority to trample on serpents and scorpions, and over all the power of the enemy, and nothing shall by any means hurt you"* (Luke 10:19). This is why we can speak with authority when we speak healing over anyone who has been tormented by the devil.

Let's declare our healing right now. We are asking God to anoint this page so when you lay hands on it, you will receive healing!

I Will Bless God

Bless the LORD, O my soul,
and forget not all His benefits:
who forgives all your iniquities,
who heals all your diseases.

PSALM 103:2–3

Father, I praise you for being the God who loves us so much that you even remind us in your Word not to forget *all* your benefits! Father, don't ever let me forget a single one of them because I rejoice with open arms to receive all the blessings you want me to have! I thank you that all my sins are gone, gone, gone. You have healed *all* my diseases. I'm walking in divine health, and I praise you for that! Thank you for redeeming my life from the pit of corruption and for beautifying me with your loving kindness and tender mercies!

God's Word Heals Me

He sent His word and healed them,
and delivered them from their destructions.
PSALM 107:20

Thank you, Father, for sending your Word to heal us. Thank you that there is no sickness in your kingdom, and we don't have to be in bondage to disease and illness. I love you, Father, because the prescription to heal every disease is written in your Word! We're delivered from all of our destructions and healed of all our physical problems. Thank you for sending your Word of healing and deliverance. Thank you for your unfailing words of all your good promises—in the past, the present, and the future! I love you and worship you for that!

I Listen Carefully

*He said, "If you listen carefully to the L*ORD *your God and do what is right in his eyes, if you pay attention to his commands and keep all his decrees, I will not bring on you any of the diseases I brought on the Egyptians, for I am the L*ORD*, who heals you."*
EXODUS 15:26, NIV

I'm listening carefully, Father, and I praise you for talking long enough for me to hear your voice and for keeping your Holy Spirit constantly after me so that I will do what is right. Thank you for my ears that hear, and thank you for the promise that you won't put any of the diseases of the Egyptians upon me. Thank you, Lord, you bring good news and healing! I praise you for being a disease-free God!

Jesus Heals Me

But He was wounded for our transgressions,
He was bruised for our iniquities;
the chastisement for our peace was upon Him,
and by His stripes we are healed.

ISAIAH 53:5

I thank you, Father, for your wonderful Word of prophecy through Isaiah, as he predicted the suffering of your Son years before it happened! Thank you for the wounds that covered our transgressions. How I love Jesus for taking the bruises for our iniquities and the chastisement of our peace! Thank you, Jesus, because those stripes on your back were taken for my healing. I am healed because of the miracle of miracles that took place over 2,000 years ago.

I Am Free from Sickness or Infirmity

That it might be fulfilled which was spoken by Isaiah the prophet, saying: "He Himself took our infirmities and bore our sicknesses."
MATTHEW 8:17

How I bless you and praise you, Father, because Jesus took every one of my infirmities, and he accepted all of this sickness upon himself. I praise you, Father, that he didn't leave some of them out, but instead, he took all the sicknesses in the entire world and bore each and every one of them for us. Now don't have to bear sickness because there's no point in both of us having it. I'm not accepting sickness in my body. It has no right here! Jesus' sacrifice was for my complete healing.

My Flesh Is Healthy

My son, give attention to my words;
incline your ear to my sayings.
Do not let them depart from your eyes;
keep them in the midst of your heart;
for they are life to those who find them,
and health to all their flesh.

PROVERBS 4:20–22

Father, I'm listening! I'm attending to your Word. I've got my ear turned to you and tuned into you. I've got my eyes glued to your words, and I'm not going to let them get out of my sight. I'm feeding on your Word so it becomes a vital part of me, right in the midst of my heart! I praise you for the life that you have given to me through your Word and for the health which I'm enjoying every day. I thank you, Father!

Healing Is Mine

He personally carried our sins in his body on the cross
so that we can be dead to sin and live for what is
right. By his wounds you are healed.
1 PETER 2:24, NLT

Thank you, Father, for the cross where Jesus died.
He took upon Himself all of our sins so that I don't
have a sin left against me. He took each and every
one of them and bore them so I can live in your
righteousness. How I love you for giving us that
health through those stripes He endured. Now I can
say, "Healing is mine!" with full confidence. Father,
I praise you! I confess these words over and over
again, "By His stripes I was healed! By His stripes I
was healed! By His stripes I was healed!" Hallelujah!

My Prayers Are Heard

*Thus says the L*ORD*, the God of David your father:*
"I have heard your prayer, I have seen your tears; surely
I will heal you."

2 KINGS 20:5

Heavenly Father, thank you for looking down at me and seeing my tears—all of them. I praise you that not a single one of them has escaped you. Thank you for your promise to heal me. I love you, Father, from the innermost recesses of my heart. I thank you because you have heard my prayers. Whether eloquently spoken or poorly worded, you hear my prayers and you will heal me.

All Sickness Must Leave My Body

And the LORD will take away from you all sickness, and will afflict you with none of the terrible diseases of Egypt which you have known, but will lay them on all those who hate you.

DEUTERONOMY 7:15

Father, I'm healed before I get sick! Hallelujah! I praise you, Father, for taking away from me all illness and disease. You love and protect those who are faithful to you. Thank you, Father, because your Word promises that you take away from me *all sickness* and not just some sicknesses. I rejoice in the wonderful health you have given me, heavenly Father!

My Heart Is Happy and Healthy

A merry heart does good, like medicine,
but a broken spirit dries the bones.
PROVERBS 17:22

Father, I'm laughing right now! You said that laughter does me good like a medicine. I thank you for that dose of heavenly medicine, and now I'm going to laugh all day long because a merry heart brings healing like a medicine. Thank you for letting me know that I should have a good sense of humor. Thank you that I don't have to have a depressed mind or a broken spirit, which dries up my bones. You have renewed me! Thank you that we can give my brothers and sisters in Christ a dose of medicine when they need it by cheering their hearts with laughter.

God's Will for Me Is Divine Health

When He had come down from the mountain, great multitudes followed Him. And behold, a leper came and worshiped Him, saying, "Lord, if You are willing, You can make me clean." Then Jesus put out His hand and touched him, saying, "I am willing; be cleansed." Immediately his leprosy was cleansed.

MATTHEW 8:1-3

Jesus, thank you that you are willing to heal me and you are healing me. I love you because you *want* me to have all the good things in life. I bless you because your Word tells me that Jesus has no desire for me to be sick. You want to heal me! I praise you, Father, because you are a God who wants us in perfect and divine health!

Nothing Is Too Hard for God

*Behold, I am the L*ORD*, the God of all flesh.*
Is there anything too hard for Me?
JEREMIAH 32:27

Father, you are the God of *all* flesh! I praise you because you never do things halfway; you always go all the way and finish what you started! I love you, Father! I'm so glad that nothing is too hard for you! When my own situations become so big and they overwhelm me, I can give them to you and rest safe and secure in the knowledge that *nothing* is too hard for you. Father, I worship you because my insurmountable mountains are stacks of children's blocks to you that can easily be knocked over. Because of this, I give you all my troubles. Hallelujah!

God Is with Me

*Then shall your light break forth like the dawn,
and your healing shall spring up speedily; your
righteousness shall go before you; the glory of the LORD
shall be your rear guard. Then you shall call, and
the LORD will answer; you shall cry, and he will say,
"Here I am."*

ISAIAH 58:8-9

Thank you, Father, for the glorious light you shed upon me. I thank you for your promises of healing and restoration. Your godliness leads me forward and your goodness is just like a shield for me, bringing me peace and prosperity. You're always there when I call, and thank you that you so quickly reply, "I am here!" Glory, Father, I'm overcome with your promises! Thank you for removing every form of false and wicked speaking and for guiding me continually!

I Will Have a Long Life

The fear of the LORD prolongs days,
but the years of the wicked will be shortened.
PROVERBS 10:27

Heavenly Father, I praise you that my life is long. I love you and stand in awe of your majesty and greatness, and because of this, you lengthen my days. I praise you for shortening the days of the wicked. I rejoice that I have favor with you. You bless my days with health and peace of mind. You reward the lives of the righteous. Thank you for always blessing me with all the good things in life. I love you!

My Words Promote Health

There is one who speaks like the piercings of a sword,
but the tongue of the wise promotes health.
PROVERB 12:18

Father, you have given me a wise tongue and have taught me to speak divine health. You've taught me not to let any corrupt communication come out of my mouth and not to acknowledge the sickness of the devil. Instead, I confidently say, "I'm catching a healing," when the devil tries to give me a cold. Father, I praise you because my own tongue brings your health into my life! I bless you for this! I thank you that a wise tongue speaks your Word, which brings healing to my body. Thank you for harnessing my tongue to bring it under control!

My Words Are a Tree of Life

A wholesome tongue is a tree of life,
but perverseness in it breaks the spirit.
PROVERBS 15:4

Father, my tongue is wholesome! You are the one who has made this possible. I thank you that my tongue is a tree of life that brings health and happiness. Because you control my tongue, I don't break down my spirit with contrary words. I give up the griping that brings discouragement and speak words that are gentle and have healing power. My tongue is wholesome and brings wholeness into my life. I love you for this, Father.

God Takes Away Sickness

Worship the LORD your God,
and his blessing will be on your food and water.
I will take away sickness from among you,
and none will miscarry or be barren in your land.
I will give you a full life span.
EXODUS 23:25–26

I praise you, Father, that my bread is blessed and so is my water. I thank you because you have taken sickness away from me and my family. I praise you, Father, for making abundant life flow all over my land during my entire lifetime! Glory!

My Heart Retains God's Words

He also taught me, and said to me:
"Let your heart retain my words;
Keep my commands, and live."
PROVERBS 4:4

Father, I love you and praise you because your words are written in my heart. I'm keeping them there by memorizing and declaring them, and I know what your Word says. I'm keeping your commandments. Thank you, Father, that your Word has told me if I do this I will have a long and happy life. I'm holding fast to every word you have said. I'm declaring all of your promises, and I'm hiding them in the deepest recesses of my heart so that I won't sin against you, Father! I keep your commandments and I am living abundantly.

God Restored My Heart

He heals the brokenhearted
and binds up their wounds.

PSALM 147:3

Father, even though my heart has been broken, you put it back together again. Thank you that you didn't leave me to gather up the pieces, but you gathered them all up for me and put them together to make my heart whole again. Your loving care is curing all my pains and all my sorrows. Thank you for those divine bandages with that everlasting healing power in them that you wrap around all of my wounds. Hallelujah, Father, I love you for that!

I Repent and My Sins Are Forgiven

And the prayer of faith will save the sick,
and the Lord will raise him up.
And if he has committed sins, he will be forgiven.

JAMES 5:15

Heavenly Father, thank you because I can pray for myself, and I can also have others pray for me because you said the "prayer of faith" will heal the sick. Father, I praise you when I am too sick to pray for myself that I can depend on my friends and brothers and sisters in Christ to pray the prayer of faith for me. Thank you for raising me from my sick bed, and if there's any sin in my life, you forgive me. Father, I praise you for the most wonderful life in the world: a life following Jesus.

I Will Live a Divine Life

*I shall not die, but live,
and declare the works of the LORD.*
PSALM 118:17

I praise you, glorious Father, for your Word that you have given us to stand on. Your works are truly magnificent and wonderful! If the doctors tell me I have an incurable disease and that there is nothing they can do, I will declare your Word over my body and know that I shall not die, but live, proclaiming your wonderful works. Thank you, Father, for your positive promises, which give hope to the weakest in heart. Father, I boldly declare your works! Glory!

I Will Leap with Strength and Joy

But for you who fear my name, the sun of righteousness shall rise with healing in its wings. You shall go out leaping like calves from the stall.
MALACHI 4:2, ESV

Father, I bless and praise you because there's healing in the wings of the Sun of Righteousness. I praise the blessings in His wings, and one of them is healing. Thank you for setting me free so I can leap and dance with joy! Father, no worldly joy compares with the joy I have because of the healing in those wings. I continually praise, respect, and have awe for your name because of your good promises to all of your children!

God Heals My Wounds

*"I will give you back your health
and heal your wounds,"* says the LORD.
JEREMIAH 30:17, NLT

You will restore health to me, Father! I praise you because you didn't say you would have to think about it. You simply said that you would restore health to me. Thank you that you heal me of all my wounds in my body, mind, and spirit. I rejoice because I can worship you and serve you as a whole, healthy person. Father, thank you for giving me your best promises! You are the best promise-giver and the best promise-keeper in the entire world.

God Strengthens My Bones

Do not be wise in your own eyes;
Fear the LORD and turn away from evil.
It will be healing to your body
and refreshment to your bones.
PROVERBS 3:7–8, NASB

Father, I don't have to be smart in my own eyes. I worship you. I praise you. I love you. I adore you, and because of you, I turn entirely away from all sin and evil. Thank you, Father, that because you taught me this, I have health to my nerves and sinews and life-giving blood in the marrow of my bones. Thank you that my bones aren't dry and brittle but are moist and pliable. I reach out and accept your gift of health! I love you, Father!

God Blesses My Household

*Blessed are all who fear the LORD, who walk in
obedience to him. You will eat the fruit of your
labor; blessings and prosperity will be yours. Your wife
will be like a fruitful vine within your house; your
children will be like olive shoots around your table. Yes,
this will be the blessing for the man who fears the LORD.*

PSALM 128:1-4, NIV

Thank you, Father, that my family and I have
your blessings and we walk in obedience to your
Word. I praise you for healthy children! You reward
me on this earth by giving me children as strong
and healthy as young olive trees. Thank you, Father,
for including healthy children in your promise
reward of prosperity and happiness to those who
love and serve you. I love to tell my children that
it's you, our Father in heaven, who blesses, protects,
and prospers us! Thank you, Father!

My Eyes and Ears Are Open

The eyes of those who see will not be dim,
and the ears of those who hear will listen.

ISAIAH 32:3

Father, I praise you that you have given me eyes that see and ears that hear, for your Word says that I have them. Because my eyes are not dim in spiritual matters, I am not fooled by the devil's temptations. Because my ears are not deaf in spiritual things, I am not deceived by the devil's lies. I see and hear correctly because you have blessed me with physical health and spiritual discernment, and I praise you for that, Father. You are a wonderful God, who is loving, merciful, and powerful!

God Safeguards My Household

No evil shall befall you,
nor shall any plague come near your dwelling.
PSALM 91:10

Thank you, Father, for protecting me from all illness and disease. Your Word promises that you won't let any evil or plague overtake me. I thank you for protection from colds, flu, infections, and plagues of any kind. Father, you are my physician, and you have the best hospitalization plan in the world, which is for us to stay healthy! You can heal anything that befalls me, and I love you for keeping me healthy so I don't have to get healed! Thank you for divine health! Thank you for that divine protection from accidents too. Thank you for that barrier around me that protects me from wicked tongues. Thank you for protection of *all* kinds.

God Spoke Life into Me

And when I passed by you and saw you struggling in your own blood, I said to you in your blood, "Live!" Yes, I said to you in your blood, "Live!"

EZEKIEL 16:6

Father, thank you for protection. I praise and thank you because when my blood flows from me during an attack from the devil, I can stand on the rock of your Word. I know that you say, "Live," to me. Thank you for loving me so much that you want me to be healthy, whole, and protected throughout my body. I praise you, heavenly Father, when I see a brother or sister in distress or trouble from bleeding, I can use your Word and command hemorrhaging to stop. I love you, Father!

God's Glory Protects Me

So shall they fear the name of the LORD from the west, and His glory from the rising of the sun; when the enemy comes in like a flood, the Spirit of the LORD will lift up a standard against him.

ISAIAH 59:19

How I thank you, Father, for your constant protection of my health and well being. Thank you for letting me know that the enemy will try to attack me over and over, but when he does and it seems as though I might be swept under, your Spirit is always there to put up a barrier against him. I praise you for your protection, your constant care, and your loving-kindness from the rising of the sun until it goes down.

God Hears Me When I Cry Out

O LORD my God, I cried out to You,
and You have healed me.
PSALM 30:2

Father, how I praise you that when my health dwindles or even seems to be gone completely, I can cry out to you and you heal me! I love you, Father, because when I get wounded in the battle of health, no matter how deep or painful those wounds are you have promised in your Word to heal me. I praise you, Father, because things that are impossible with men are possible with you! You are a God of love, truth, and victory, and I rejoice in your miraculous healing power and glorify you for it! Thank you for another month of victorious health. I continue to trust you and your loving kindness. Thank you that all the promises I've declared this month are true! Hallelujah!

OCTOBER

The Holy Spirit

October is the month of *power*! Jesus told His disciples to go and preach the gospel to every creature. Then He immediately put up a stop sign and said, "Wait!" He told them to go in the upper room and wait for the Holy Spirit because He knew they were powerless without the Holy Spirit.

The minute the disciples received the baptism of the Holy Spirit and began speaking in other tongues, they began to preach about Jesus and glorified Him. Once you have the baptism of the Holy Spirit, your focus will be on Jesus.

If you've never received the power of the Christian life, which is the baptism of the Holy Spirit, you *will*, after declaring the Word written this month on the Holy Spirit!

I Have Power

But you shall receive power when the Holy Spirit has come upon you; and you shall be witnesses to Me in Jerusalem, and in all Judea and Samaria, and to the end of the earth.

ACTS 1:8

I have power because your wonderful Word says so! I have ability, efficiency, and might because of your Holy Spirit! I thank you that the Holy Spirit not only fills me, but is completely diffused throughout my very soul! How I praise you for completely immersing and submerging me in the power of your Holy Spirit! You have given me the boldness of a lion to speak and share the Good News at all times. I'm talking to my neighbors. I'm talking to my fellow employees. I'm talking to the people I do business with! Father, I'm so bold today. I am your witness wherever I go today.

God Gives Me Good Gifts

If you then, being evil, know how to give good gifts
to your children, how much more will your heavenly
Father give the Holy Spirit to those who ask Him!
LUKE 11:13

I thank you, Father, that you never give me anything evil. I love you and praise you because everything you give to me is good. I always want to give the best to my children, and I thank you, Father, that you want to give the best to me. I'm so glad that you love me more than I could ever love a member of my family, and that you give me better gifts than I could ever hope to give my loved ones. I am loved by you and you have given me the gift of your precious Holy Spirit. Thank you that I don't have to speculate or wonder if it's good or evil. I have complete certainty that all your gifts are good because they are from you!

I Am Filled
with the Spirit

And suddenly there came a sound from heaven, as of a rushing mighty wind, and it filled the whole house where they were sitting. Then there appeared to them divided tongues, as of fire, and one sat upon each of them. And they were all filled with the Holy Spirit and began to speak with other tongues, as the Spirit gave them utterance.

ACTS 2:2–4

Heavenly Father, I love you because the rushing sound that came on the day of Pentecost came right from heaven! I thank you that it fell upon *all* of those present and that they were *all* filled with the Holy Spirit and began to speak in tongues as the Spirit gave them utterance. I thank you, Father, because you haven't changed your plan and you don't restrict the Holy Spirit to just a few, but you give it to *all* of us. Father, I praise you for loving me just as much as you loved the disciples, and for giving me the same beautiful gift of the Holy Spirit.

I Am on Fire for God

I baptize you with water for repentance, but he who is coming after me is mightier than I, whose sandals I am not worthy to carry. He will baptize you with the Holy Spirit and fire.

MATTHEW 3:11, ESV

I'm on fire, Father, and I want to keep this fire burning! I praise you that your promises have come down through the ages so that I could receive the same baptism that the disciples did on the day of Pentecost! The fire of the Holy Spirit burns out the chaff in my life, but is a fire that cannot be put out or burned out! I bless you and praise you because this indwelling power enables me to live above the sin of the world with a complete distaste for the things of the world! Jesus, you are mighty and you baptize me with the Holy Spirit and fire.

I Walk in the Spirit of God

Walk in the Spirit,
and you shall not fulfill the lust of the flesh.
GALATIANS 5:16

I'm walking and leaping and praising God in the Spirit! Thank you, Father, for making your Word so simple for me to understand. I'm responsive to, controlled, and guided by your Holy Spirit, and I'm walking, talking, and living in the Spirit at all times. You alone empower me to do this because you enable me to look at the lust of the flesh without gratifying those desires, which are of my human nature and not of you. I don't have to listen to the devil when he talks to me, because I'm walking in the Spirit—in power and glory, overcoming the devil all the way! How I praise and love you!

I Am in God's Perfect Will

In the same way, the Spirit helps us in our weakness. We do not know what we ought to pray for, but the Spirit himself intercedes for us through wordless groans. And he who searches our hearts knows the mind of the Spirit, because the Spirit intercedes for God's people in accordance with the will of God.

ROMANS 8:26–27, NIV

Father, your Spirit is helping me to pray according to your perfect will. I bless you for giving me such a beautiful prayer language with which to pray. When my burdens are great and I don't know what to say, I pray in the Spirit and He intercedes and makes intercession for me. In the Spirit I always pray in perfect harmony with your perfect will. I praise you, Father, that the Holy Spirit rushes to my aid at all times!

I Am Not a Fool

Therefore do not be foolish,
but understand what the will of the Lord is.
And do not get drunk with wine,
for that is debauchery,
but be filled with the Spirit.
EPHESIANS 5:17–18, ESV

Father, I'm filled up all the way to the top and running over with your Spirit! I praise you for letting me be wise in your ways so I will know what your will is. Thank you for telling me not to be drunk with wine. I praise you because my spirit can now soar higher and be stimulated more with the new wine of the Spirit than it ever can on artificial means. Father, I love you for giving me power to know your will!

The Holy Spirit
Is My Helper

*But the Helper, the Holy Spirit, whom the Father will
send in My name, He will teach you all things, and
bring to your remembrance all things
that I said to you.*
JOHN 14:26

Father, thank you that the Holy Spirit is the
Comforter, Counselor, Helper, Intercessor, Advocate,
Strengthener, and Standby in all situations. I thank
you that the Holy Spirit was sent to magnify Jesus.
I thank you for not limiting the Holy Spirit in
teaching me certain truths, but for sending Him to
teach me all things, and to bring *all* of what your
Word says to my remembrance. Thank you, Father,
that I can trust what the Holy Spirit brings to my
mind because it is *all* good, and *all* from you. Thank
you for being so good to me!

I Drink God's Living Water

But whoever drinks of the water that I shall give him will never thirst. But the water that I shall give him will become in him a fountain of water springing up into everlasting life.

JOHN 4:14

I'm drinking at the springs of living water and I'm happy! I never get parched and thirsty as long as I continue to drink from that water. I thank you and praise you that you are a well within my soul that springs up into everlasting life. Father, I praise you for taking me out of the dry years I spent with the devil, and you put me where I shall never thirst again. Thank you for that well of water, which is constantly welling up, flowing, and bubbling within me unto eternal life.

The Holy Spirit Is with Me Always

And I will pray the Father, and He will give you another Helper, that He may abide with you forever.
JOHN 14:16

Father, I love you, I love you, I love you for giving me another Helper. Even more than that, Father, I praise you because you have promised that He will abide with me forever. I praise you and thank you that the Holy Spirit is abiding in me right now, helping, comforting, and accompanying me wherever I go. I praise you, Father, that the Holy Spirit is the Spirit of Truth. I receive your truth, which is alive in my heart and guiding my every step!

I Walk with the Spirit of Truth

But when the Helper comes, whom I shall send to you from the Father, the Spirit of truth who proceeds from the Father, He will testify of Me.

JOHN 15:26

Thank you, Father, that the Holy Spirit testifies to me about Jesus. I praise you that the Holy Spirit is the Spirit of Truth who rightly divides that which is the true from the false. I can always depend on the Holy Spirit to reveal the truth to me in all situations in the world, and also in your Word. I praise you, Father, that the Holy Spirit comes from you and not from the devil. I praise you, Jesus, that the Holy Spirit is constantly reminding me at all times of you, your love for me, your sacrifice, and your cleansing power. I thank you that the Holy Spirit is also the Counselor, Helper, Advocate, Intercessor, and Strengthener!

The Holy Spirit Was Poured Out for Me

And afterward, I will pour out my Spirit on all people.
Your sons and daughters will prophesy,
your old men will dream dreams,
your young men will see visions.

JOEL 2:28, NIV

Father, I praise you that you are pouring out your Spirit upon all flesh. I praise you that this includes me and I thank you for pouring it all over me. Thank you for giving us the ability to dream dreams, have visions, and prophesy. I thank you and praise you, Father, because your Spirit is a blessing to me more than ever before. I praise you that you didn't restrict your Holy Spirit to some, but that you freely give to all who ask. So I ask, fill me with your Spirit afresh today.

God Helps Me Overcome Evil

Therefore, brethren, we are debtors—not to the flesh, to live according to the flesh. For if you live according to the flesh you will die; but if by the Spirit you put to death the deeds of the body, you will live.

ROMANS 8:12–13

Father, I thank you that I am not a debtor to the flesh, and therefore I don't have to live after the lust of the flesh. I thank you and praise you, Father, that through the power of the Spirit, I am constantly putting to death the evil deeds prompted by the flesh so that I may live! I thank you that it gets easier every day for me to turn from my carnal nature. I am putting to death the evil deeds through the power of the Holy Spirit.

I Have the Fruit of the Spirit

But the fruit of the Spirit is love, joy, peace, longsuffering, kindness, goodness, faithfulness, gentleness, self-control. Against such there is no law.
GALATIANS 5:22–23

I rejoice and praise you, Father, for your love in my heart. The fruit of the Spirit is abundant in my life and you give me what I have not had before. I can love the unlovely! I am running over with joy and peace and longsuffering. I praise you for gentleness, goodness, and faith. I thank you for meekness and self-control. I love you for giving me not just one of the fruits of the Spirit, but *all* of them! The fruit of your Spirit is abundant in my life.

I Am Led by the Spirit of God

For as many as are led by the Spirit of God, these are sons of God. For you did not receive the spirit of bondage again to fear, but you received the Spirit of adoption by whom we cry out, "Abba, Father."

ROMANS 8:14–15

I am a child of God! Father, I love you for leading me by your Spirit and for making me your child! I praise you for your Word, which assures me that I won't be left out. You say *as many as are led*, and not just a selected few, are the children of God. Thank you that I'm not caught up in slavery to fear, but instead I've been adopted into your very own family! I rejoice and thank you for the presence and power of your Holy Spirit, which enables me to do the greater things your Word promises! I have received the spirit of adoption and cry out, "Abba, Father."

God's Light Shines in Me

We now have this light shining in our hearts, but we ourselves are like fragile clay jars containing this great treasure. This makes it clear that our great power is from God, not from ourselves.

2 CORINTHIANS 4:7, NLT

I praise and thank you, Father, for the light inside my physical body that is right this minute shining out of me upon the world. The divine light of your gospel shines so brightly that it's evident it isn't from my own power, but yours illuminated through me. I praise you Father, for making me a powerful floodlight that shows the lost ones how to find you! I rejoice because the whole world can see that the grandeur and exceeding greatness of power and glory are yours!

God's Power Makes Me Victorious

Since you seek a proof of Christ speaking in me,
who is not weak toward you, but mighty in you.
For though He was crucified in weakness, yet He lives
by the power of God. For we also are weak in Him,
but we shall live with Him by the power
of God toward you.

2 CORINTHIANS 13:3–4

All of God's power is mine! Heavenly Father, how I praise you that Jesus is powerful within me. I thank you that His human body died on a cross but He was resurrected, and that He now lives by the mighty power of your Spirit. I thank you that even when we are weak in our bodies, we have your power to use to make our lives victorious at all times! Thank you, Father, for this divine privilege.

I Have the Mind of Christ

For to us God revealed them through the Spirit;
for the Spirit searches all things,
even the depths of God.
1 CORINTHIANS 2:10, NASB

Father, I thank you that you have revealed the secrets of the universe to us by and through your Holy Spirit. I praise you that the Spirit searches everything completely, thoroughly, effectually, wholly, and in every respect. You have made all of the things that are beyond man's scrutiny and investigation available to me! I praise you, Father, that because I have the mind of Christ, these deep truths are available to me!

I Have Discernment

The natural person does not accept the things of the Spirit of God, for they are folly to him, and he is not able to understand them because they are spiritually discerned. The spiritual person judges all things, but is himself to be judged by no one.

1 CORINTHIANS 2:14–15, ESV

I am not a natural or unspiritual man, Father! I am a spiritual person who can receive *all* of the wonderful things from the Spirit. I welcome and accept the wonderful gifts and teachings of the Holy Spirit. Father, you let me investigate and appraise all things because I am a spiritual man— because your Word says so! I praise you, Father, that even though I judge all things and all situations, I am judged by no one!

I Will Pray in the Spirit

*What is the conclusion then? I will pray with the
spirit, and I will also pray with the understanding.
I will sing with the spirit, and I will also sing with the
understanding.*

1 CORINTHIANS 14:15

Father, I thank you that I can pray and praise
you with my mind and understanding, and I can
also pray and praise you with my spirit through
the power of the Holy Spirit! When I have feelings
in my heart that can't be expressed because they
are overwhelming, you give me a special way to
pray and praise you with my spirit to express those
feelings! I thank you that I don't have to confine
my singing to my understanding, but that my spirit
can sing also!

I Speak with a Heavenly Language

For he who speaks in a tongue does not speak to men but to God, for no one understands him; however, in the spirit he speaks mysteries.

1 CORINTHIANS 14:2

Thank you, Father, that you have given me an unknown tongue with which to praise you. This special language is a private, personal, distinctive, and unique communication that I have with you. Others can't understand it, but you can, Father. I praise you that in the spirit I can utter secret truths and hidden things to you. Your Spirit understands my spirit and answers! Thank you, Father, for the mysteries my spirit converses with you. You answer my prayers even before I utter them from my mouth.

I Sing in a Heavenly Language

And the spirits of the prophets
are subject to the prophets.
1 CORINTHIANS 14:32

Father, I praise you that you give me control over my own spirit. The Holy Spirit does not force me to do anything I don't want to do. I thank you, Father, that you have stored in my human body the power of the Holy Spirit, so that I can pray in tongues any time I want to, and I can stop praying in tongues any time I want to. I love you for this, Father. Thank you for the glorious privilege of singing in tongues and then stopping whenever I choose!

I Keep the Commandments

Now he who keeps His commandments abides in Him, and He in him. And by this we know that He abides in us, by the Spirit whom He has given us.

1 JOHN 3:24

I thank you and praise you, glorious Father, for I know that you abide in me because of the Spirit which you have given to me. Thank you, Father, that I don't have to wonder or question whether or not I belong to you because your very own Spirit within me testifies to me that you dwell in me. You have given me this positive proof that I am your child. I bless you, Father, for telling me that you dwell, reside, live, stay, and abide in me, which means you accept me. Glory to you, Father, for such a great gift.

I Drink from God's Fountain

And the Spirit and the bride say, "Come!"
And let him who hears say, "Come!"
And let him who thirsts come.
Whoever desires, let him take the water of life freely.

REVELATION 22:17

Father, you said whoever desires may come and take of the water of life freely. I want your living water and I drink at the fountain of life. Thank you that your Spirit called me; thank you that you're not stingy with the flow of that fountain. You said that I can just drink and drink and drink! Father, I love your living water, and I love you for giving from a bountiful supply! My heart is overflowing with gratitude and joy because of the wonderful things you say in your Word. I praise you that my soul is constantly refreshed, supported, and strengthened by it!

God Gives Me the Right Words

When you are brought before synagogues, rulers and authorities, do not worry about how you will defend yourselves or what you will say, for the Holy Spirit will teach you at that time what you should say.

LUKE 12:11-12, NIV

How I praise and thank you, Father, that when I run into situations where I find it difficult to speak what is on my heart and I don't know the answers, your Holy Spirit teaches me quickly and wisely exactly what I need to say! I thank you that I don't have to be anxious or worried, but that I can always depend on your beautiful Holy Spirit to teach me the right words to say under all conditions.

God is Faithful to Me

No temptation has overtaken you except such as is common to man; but God is faithful, who will not allow you to be tempted beyond what you are able, but with the temptation will also make the way of escape, that you may be able to bear it.

1 CORINTHIANS 10:13

Father, how I bless you for your Word. No enticement to sin, no matter where it comes from or where it leads to, will overcome me beyond human resistance because of your compassionate nature and understanding. I praise you because I can trust you to always provide the way out so that I can be capable, strong, and powerful to overcome whatever temptation comes my way. Father, because of your faithfulness to me, I shall be faithful to you and depend on your Word to keep me from falling into ditches that lie alongside the straight and narrow way.

My Words Demonstrate God's Power

And my speech and my preaching were not with persuasive words of human wisdom, but in demonstration of the Spirit and of power, that your faith should not be in the wisdom of men but in the power of God.

1 CORINTHIANS 2:4–5

Dear Father, I praise you that we don't have to be gifted orators but simply ordinary people who use your boldness to share the gospel you back up with the power of your Holy Spirit. My faith is not in the wisdom of men, but in the power of God. Your power will cause people to have faith in you. I love you, Father, for using me to further your kingdom. Hallelujah!

God Has a Barrier of Security around Me

*When the enemy comes in like a flood, the Spirit of the L*ORD *will lift up a standard against him.*
ISAIAH 59:19

Father, when the enemy roars around like a lion, I don't have to worry because your Spirit raises up a standard against him that puts him to flight! Father, I love you beyond measure because I don't have to be afraid of the devil or the evil around me. I know at all times that your Spirit drives away the enemy. Thank you, Lord, that I'm always on the winning side! Thank you that I have victory!

God is Almighty and Powerful

So he said to me, "This is the word of the Lord to
Zerubbabel: 'Not by might nor by power,
but by my Spirit,' says the Lord Almighty."

ZECHARIAH 4:6

Heavenly Father, I praise you that I don't have to be a superhero full of strength, nor a powerful individual who can shake mountains, because my battles are all won in the Spirit. I thank you, Father, that the same promise that you gave to Zerubbabel applies to me—that all things are accomplished not by might, nor by power, but by your Spirit. I rejoice, Father, because your Spirit dwells in me! I thank you, Father, that the oil of the Holy Spirit is never-ending. Hallelujah!

I Speak Words of Life

It is the Spirit who gives life;
the flesh profits nothing.
The words that I speak to you are spirit,
and they are life.

JOHN 6:63

How I praise you, Father, that it is the Holy Spirit who quickens my mind to understand the truths of your Word and other truths spoken to me. Your words are spirit and life, and I thank you that because of your Holy Spirit, your Word is alive and living in me today! I thank you that I don't have to be dead in sin the way I was, but that I now have life in the Spirit! I know that my flesh conveys no benefit, there is no heavenly profit in it, and it is your life-giving Spirit that has made me come alive in Christ. I worship and praise you for that, Father!

Nothing Can Harm Me

*And these signs will follow those who believe;
In My name they will cast out demons; they will speak
with new tongues; they will take up serpents; and if they
drink anything deadly, it will by no means hurt them;
they will lay hands on the sick, and they will recover.*

MARK 16:17–18

I'm a believer! Father, how I praise you because
you have promised that through your Holy Spirit,
signs follow me because I believe! I thank you that
I can use the name of Jesus and cast out devils and
speak with new tongues! I thank you that nothing
can harm me because your Spirit will protect
me! Because of the power of your Holy Spirit,
sick people recover when I lay hands on them!
Hallelujah! Thank you for the signs that follow me
wherever I go!

NOVEMBER

Praise and Thanksgiving

Let's make November a month of "thanks" giving—a time of great joy as we remember *all* the things to thank God for.

We thank God for Jesus, the rock of our salvation (2 Samuel 22:2). We thank God for salvation through the blood of Jesus Christ (Ephesians 1:7). We thank God for marriage (Matthew 19:6). We thank God for children (Psalm 127:4). We thank God for many blessings (Philippians 4:19). We thank God for grandchildren (Proverbs 17:6). We thank God for ministry (Ephesians 4:11–12). We thank God for His Word (Mark 13:31). We thank God for faith (Romans 12:3).

Let's declare these praise and thanksgiving declarations at least ten times each day so that our spirits will be soaring in the heavens every day this month.

I Will Always Bless God

I will bless the Lord at all times;
His praise shall continually be in my mouth.
PSALM 34:1

Bless the Lord, O my soul! All day long I bless you because of your goodness to me. I bless you because you are the magnificent Creator who put the stars in the sky and separated the land from the sea. I bless you because you always keep your promises, even when fulfilling them requires miracles! I bless you, Father, because you have lifted me out of darkness and led me to victory. I bless you and praise you for your praises are sweeter than honey in my mouth. I praise you for your faithfulness to me. I praise you, Father, because it blesses me to keep your praises continually on my lips!

My Gladness Overflows

Be glad in the Lord and rejoice, you righteous;
and shout for joy, all you upright in heart!

PSALM 32:11

Father, I'm filled to overflowing with gladness in you! I'm glad because my whole life is in your hands. I can't stop rejoicing because you have made me righteous through your glorious righteousness! You have made me upright because your strength is everlasting! I can't keep silent because if I did the very rocks would cry out. I don't want to keep silent, for my heart tells me to shout for joy! Father, I have to sing and shout for joy because you've not only given me a wonderful day today, but you've given me a wonderful future to look forward to, in this life and the next!

God Is Worthy of My Praise

Let my mouth be filled with Your praise
and with Your glory all the day.
PSALM 71:8

My mouth declares your praises, Father, because in all ways you are worthy of that praise! I honor and rejoice in your name! Father, I really want to thank you that my mouth doesn't have to be filled with mockery, scorn, contempt, complaints, deceit, and accusation. I'm so filled with joy in praising you and your goodness that the world's conversation habits don't interest me. I praise and honor you because in all the blessings you bring to me and to my family—love, joy, peace, health, and prosperity—the glory belongs to you. I honor you because you are a righteous and loving God, the fountainhead of all blessings.

I Lift Up My Heart

*It is good to give thanks to the L*ORD*,*
to sing praises to the Most High.
PSALM 92:1, NLT

Heavenly Father, I rejoice and give thanks to you because you fill my life with so many good things that I overflow with feelings of thankfulness. I praise you, Father, and I thoroughly enjoy the abundance of blessings you bring to me because of who you are! How can I not be thankful for each bite of food when I love the Provider with all my heart? It is good to give thanks to you and sing your praises because it pleases you and lifts up my heart to you. By thanking you, I send you my love. By singing your praises, I send you my love. Thank you for the joy you put in my heart.

I Will Make a Joyful Noise

Make a joyful shout to the LORD, all you lands! Serve the Lord with gladness; come before His presence with singing. Know that the LORD, He is God; it is He who has made us, and not we ourselves; we are His people and the sheep of His pasture. Enter into His gates with thanksgiving, and into His courts with praise. Be thankful to Him, and bless His name.

PSALM 100:1–4

Father, I'm making a joyful noise because I only want to talk about you and to celebrate your presence in my life with praise and thanksgiving. I serve you gladly with all my heart, mind, body, and soul. I can't stand in your presence without singing because you have made me so glad to be your child! I praise you that we can enter your gates with thanksgiving and I thank you that we can enter your courts with praise. I bless and praise you, heavenly Father.

God Rescued Me!

*I will praise You, O Lᴏʀᴅ my God, with all my heart,
and I will glorify Your name forevermore.*
PSALM 86:12

I praise you, Father, with all of my heart and
all of my being! I thank you because you made
provision for forgiveness of my sins. You saved me
from eternal death through the sacrifice of your
beloved Son. You rescued me out of the miry clay
to set my feet on solid rock. Father, I'm blessed
to sing your praises because there is so much for
which to praise you! I love you and praise you with
every part of my being. I will glorify and lift up
your holy name forever!

I Will Sing God's Praises

I will sing to the LORD as long as I live;
I will sing praise to my God while I have my being.
PSALM 104:33

Father, I thank you for the privilege of singing to you as long as I live. Singing to you is special to me, Father, because each song is an expression of thankfulness that reaches deep inside me to present an offering of joy beyond words. When I praise you in song, I feel as though you are touching me as I sing. You are lifting me up to you on the wings of that song. Heavenly Father, I thank you for listening to my songs because they always make me feel close to you. As long as there is breath in my body, I will sing praises to you!

My God Reigns!

Let the heavens rejoice,
and let the earth be glad;
and let them say among the nations,
"The LORD reigns."
1 CHRONICLES 16:31

Father, the heavens are glad, the earth rejoices, and I'm saying over and over, *the Lord reigns, the Lord reigns, the Lord reigns, the Lord reigns*! Thank you, Father, for the way my spirit leaps within me when I say these wonderful words. I praise you for putting into my heart and mouth these words that make my soul sing: *the Lord reigns*! You are the Creator and the Lord of all creation. I rejoice with the earth and join in heaven's gladness because you are my Lord and you rule over my life as well as everything else—visible and invisible! Father, I'm overwhelmed with gratitude. Even though you have so much to care for, you take wonderful care of me!

I Will Give Thanks to God

Therefore by Him let us continually offer the sacrifice of praise to God, that is, the fruit of our lips, giving thanks to His name.

HEBREWS 13:15

Father, I offer the sacrifice of praise to you continually, even though it's no sacrifice to praise you, but a wonderful privilege. I praise you continually because you bless me continually. You even bless me while I'm praising you! Father, the fruit of my lips is always good fruit in giving thanks to your name and praising you for just being who you are. Let the fruit of my lips send out the fruit of your Spirit: love, joy, peace, patience, kindness, goodness, faithfulness, gentleness, and self-control. Father, you are the God of glory, and I love to praise you!

I Will Praise God

I will praise God's name in song and glorify him with thanksgiving. This will please the LORD more than an ox, more than a bull with its horns and hooves. The poor will see and be glad—you who seek God, may your hearts live! The LORD hears the needy and does not despise his captive people. Let heaven and earth praise him, the seas and all that move in them.

PSALM 69:30–34, NIV

I praise you, Father, while I'm singing. I thank you for all the good things in life. I praise you and thank you for my family, my health, my life, and my salvation. My praise pleases you and my heart is alive with gratitude. You hear the needy and are attentive to the needs of the captive. Father, I join my voice with all the angels in heaven and people on earth and praise you with all my might!

God Hears My Praises to Him

Bless our God, O peoples;
let the sound of his praise be heard,
who has kept our soul among the living
and has not let our feet slip.

PSALM 66:8–9, ESV

Heavenly Father, I bless you and I sing, sing, sing your praises! You hold my life in your hands just as you hold all creation. I bless and thank you for that. In your hands you have everything—breath, life, and our very being. Thank you, Father, for saving, guiding, teaching, and nourishing me. You've given me not just life, but everything along with it. It's a wonderful life because you constantly show me how you want me to live and what you want me to do. You light the path in front of me, you hold my feet on that path, and you guard me from stumbling. Father, I bless you for this!

I Will Continually Praise God

*From the rising of the sun to its going down
the Lord's name is to be praised.*

PSALM 113:3

It's early in the morning, Father, and I'm praising you before I even get out of bed. I praise you because I have a warm bed to sleep in and a roof over my head. I praise you because the sun rises each day on your beautiful creation and because the flowers, grass, and trees testify to your glory. I praise you for the sunshine, for the rain, for the seasons, and for the food you put in my mouth. I praise you for all the wonderful things you give me to do each day and for opportunities to tell people about you. My lips are going to praise you this whole day long until the sun goes down. And then, Lord, I'm going to keep praising your name. Hallelujah!

I Am on the Winning Side

Jehoshaphat stood and said, "Listen to me, Judah and people of Jerusalem! Have faith in the LORD your God and you will be upheld; have faith in his prophets and you will be successful." After consulting the people, Jehoshaphat appointed men to sing to the Lord and to praise him for the splendor of his holiness as they went out at the head of the army, saying: "Give thanks to the LORD, for his love endures forever."

2 CHRONICLES 20:20–22, NIV

Father, I praise you that I am established and am prospering. I praise you for the fantastic power that there is in praise. Thank you, Father, that when the enemies came after your children, the very moment they began to sing and praise, you caused the other armies to begin fighting among themselves, and they were destroyed! Thank you, Father, that because I am your child, I'm on the winning side at all times! Hallelujah!

God Blesses My Offspring

For I will pour water on him who is thirsty,
and floods on the dry ground;
I will pour My Spirit on your descendants,
and My blessing on your offspring.

ISAIAH 44:3

Pour your water on me, Lord, because I'm thirsty! I praise you that you don't give me a tiny little straw to sip water when I'm thirsty, but you pour it all over me. There is so much that it even soaks the dry ground around me. Thank you that there is not only enough for me, but also for my offspring. I thank you that my children, and their children, are splashing in the overflow that you've given to me. I will bless you at all times, and your praise shall continually be in my mouth!

God's Love Endures Forever

The trumpeters and singers performed together in unison to praise and give thanks to the LORD. Accompanied by trumpets, cymbals, and other instruments, they raised their voices and praised the LORD with these words: "He is good! His faithful love endures forever!" At that moment a thick cloud filled the Temple of the LORD. The priests could not continue their service because of the cloud, for the glorious presence of the Lord filled the Temple of God.

2 CHRONICLES 5:13–14, NLT

Your glory surrounds praise! I praise you because the minute I begin to praise and bless you, your glory fills the temple to such an extent that at times I can't stand on my feet. Thank you, Father, that you don't reserve all the good things for heaven, but you let me have some of your glory down here! I bless you for power and majesty and glory so strong that I can't even stand up!

God's Love toward Me is Steadfast

Because your steadfast love is better than life, my lips will praise you. So I will bless you as long as I live; in your name I will lift up my hands.

PSALM 63:3–4, ESV

Father, I search for you and my soul thirsts for you. I rejoice in you, my God, because through the night you protect me in the shadow of your wings. My protection and success come from you alone. No enemy can reach me because of your love and kindness. Thank you for leading me to the mighty, towering rock of safety. I shall forever live in your tabernacle in the shelter of your wings. Thank you for all the blessings you reserve for those who call on your name!

I Seek God's Face

Oh, give thanks to the Lᴏʀᴅ! Call upon His name; make known His deeds among the peoples. Sing to Him, sing psalms to Him; talk of all His wondrous works. Glory in His holy name; let the hearts of those rejoice who seek the Lord. Seek the Lord and His strength; seek His face evermore. Remember His marvelous works which He has done, His wonders, and the judgments of His mouth.

PSALM 105:1-5

Father, I sing praises to you. I talk of all your deeds and devoutly and earnestly make them known. Father, my heart rejoices because I seek you as my indispensable necessity. I thank you that you are always there. Father, I shall seek your face all the days of my life and will remember all the wonderful and exciting deeds you have done. Hallelujah!

I Will Shout with Joy

Oh come, let us sing to the Lord! Let us shout joyfully to the Rock of our salvation. Let us come before His presence with thanksgiving; let us shout joyfully to Him with psalms. For the LORD is the great God, and the great King above all gods.

PSALM 95:1–3

I praise you, glorious Father, and sing songs before you and make a joyful noise to you because you are the Rock of my salvation. My heart wants to glorify you! I make joyful noises to you, Father, with thanksgiving in my heart and I enter before your presence with thanksgiving and songs of praise. You do so much for me that I just want to rejoice and celebrate before you! Father, I praise and thank you because you are a great God, a great King above all kings, and you are mine!

God Rescued Me

Teach me Your way, O Lord; I will walk in Your truth;
unite my heart to fear Your name. I will praise You,
O Lord my God, with all my heart, and I will glorify
Your name forevermore. For great is Your mercy toward
me, and You have delivered my soul from the depths of
Sheol.

PSALM 86:11–13

Father, I praise you for teaching me your ways so
I can avoid the deceptions of the devil and walk in
the truth. Tell me what to do and I will do it. Tell
me where you want me to go and I will go there.
Every part of my being unites in reverence and
praise to your name. With every bit of my heart, I
praise you and give glory to you. You are so kind to
me and have rescued me from deepest hell! Father,
I praise you constantly.

God Is My Jehovah, My Provider

But let the righteous be glad; let them rejoice before God; yes, let them rejoice exceedingly. Sing to God, sing praises to His name; extol Him who rides on the clouds, by His name YAH, and rejoice before Him.

PSALM 68:3–4

Heavenly Father, I am uncompromisingly righteous because of your power, and I'm glad. I jubilantly rejoice because I worship, follow, and obey the God of glory and righteousness! Father, just praising you makes my entire spirit and soul feel spirited. My mouth is filled with your praise and your honor all day long, for you are the Lord of creation, the great God over the heavens. I sing your praises because my tongue can't keep still in my mouth. I love you so much. Father, I rejoice before you—Jehovah is your name!

I Serve an Awesome God

Oh, clap your hands, all you peoples! Shout to God with the voice of triumph! For the LORD Most High is awesome; He is a great King over all the earth.

PSALM 47:1-2

Father, I clap, clap, clap my hands and rejoice with all my heart and all my mind. I shout triumphant praises to you, for you are the Lord above all lords, the God above all gods. You are awesome beyond words. The nations rise and fall at your command. All the presidents, kings, premiers, and other world leaders have their power only because you allow it. Kings and kingdoms come and go, but your reign is forever, heavenly Father. I praise you because your power is exercised in righteousness and love toward all your people. Father, I thank you, praise you, and shout praises to you because of who you are! Glory!

I Have Victory

Blessed be the LORD! For he has heard the voice of my pleas for mercy. The LORD is my strength and my shield; in him my heart trusts, and I am helped; my heart exults, and with my song I give thanks to him. The LORD is the strength of his people; he is the saving refuge of his anointed.

PSALM 28:6–8, ESV

I bless you, Father, because you hear me whenever I cry out to you for help. I praise you because you are my entire strength in time of need, my impenetrable shield in time of danger. You are with me always, and I fear no evil, not even the devil himself! I relax and my tensions disappear because I trust, rely on, and confidently lean on you. Father, you never let me down. Because I am victorious in you, my heart is filled with joy and I sing your praises!

I Have Everlasting Joy

I will declare Your name to My brethren;
in the midst of the congregation I will praise You.
PSALM 22:22

I'll gladly praise you and talk about you to my friends and relatives, Father. You'll be there to soften their hearts and open their ears. I'll praise you as they consider your Word and praise you when they finally accept your Word. When they come to know you as I know you, Father, they'll want to praise you too! I will even stand up in front of the congregation, Father, and tell about all the wonderful things you have done. I will publicly declare my testimony in the presence of those who love you and worship you. I'll praise you in the midst of them. My heart rejoices with everlasting joy and I worship you.

My God Is Wonderful

*Then each one's praise
will come from God.*
1 CORINTHIANS 4:5B

Father, I praise you that on the very special day when I stand before you in judgment, you will examine the secret places of my heart. At that time, praise will be turned around and you will give to us praise and commendation for the things I have done on earth! Father, on that day I with thank you in person for all the wonderful things you did for me on this earth! But your Word also says you're going to thank *me*! I rejoice at the thought of that wonderful day to come!

I Am a Winner in Christ

In God I have put my trust,
I will not be afraid.
What can man do to me?
Vows made to You are binding upon me, O God;
I will render praises to You.

PSALM 56:11–12

Father, I praise you and thank you because my trust is entirely in you and not in my own strength. With you as my fortress, I'm not going to fear what any man can do to me. Criticism and ridicule can't harm me, for I am shielded by your truth. Enemies can't touch me, for you confound, confuse, and defeat them by your strength. I rejoice that vows made to you are binding upon me, Father. In your strength, power, and faithfulness, my victory is assured in all circumstances! Because I trust you with all my heart, you've made me a winner. Father, I sing your praises!

I Am a Mighty One!

Give unto the LORD, O you mighty ones,
give unto the LORD glory and strength.
Give unto the LORD the glory due to His name;
worship the LORD in the beauty of holiness.

PSALM 29:1–2

Thank you, Father, that I can come before you with praise, giving you the glory and strength you deserve for all you have done and are doing for your people. I glorify you, Father, for passing on to me the inheritance of Abraham. I glorify you for giving me your Word, so that I can find instruction and understanding. I glorify you for my salvation and the blessings that go with it. You are a mighty God and you deserve all glory! I see that your holiness is glorious and I rejoice to worship you.

I Will Tell of What God Has Done

*Sing praises to the L*ORD*, who dwells in Zion;*
  Declare among the peoples His deeds.
For He who requires blood remembers them;
  He does not forget the cry of the afflicted.
PSALM 9:11–12, NASB

I praise you, Father, and sing your praises around the world! My tongue just won't keep still, but breaks out in songs of praise. You always hear me when I call to you, no matter what kind of trouble I am in. I praise you, Father, for your love and power. Your deeds, on behalf of your people, include many miracles, signs, and wonders. You hear and remember the cry of the afflicted. I will tell the world about them so that your name is glorified among all the people of the earth!

God Is My Deliverer

I will love You, O Lord, my strength. The Lord is my
rock and my fortress and my deliverer; my God, my
strength, in whom I will trust; my shield and the horn
of my salvation, my stronghold. I will call upon the
Lord, who is worthy to be praised; so shall I be saved
from my enemies.

PSALM 18:1-3

How I love you, heavenly Father, because of all
the tremendous things you have done for me. I
praise you because you provide all that I need for
my life. You are my rock, for I stand on the truth of
your Word. You are my fortress, for I am safe in you.
You are my strength, for I am victorious in you.
You are my high tower, for I have wisdom in you.
You are my deliverer, my salvation, and my God.
Without you, I would be lost in sin and darkness. I
praise you, Father, for saving me from my enemies
and lifting me into your marvelous light.

I Will Sing and Dance for God

Let them praise His name with the dance; let them sing praises to Him with the timbrel and harp.

PSALM 149:3

Father, I praise you with my strutting. I praise you for creating dancing as a form of worship to you. Sometimes, Father, I get so filled with rejoicing in you and your music, I just have to clap my hands and move my feet! You love to hear my voice and see me dance before you. I sing your praises while I dance. I use instruments to praise you even more and glorify your name!

I Will Make a Joyful Noise

Praise Him with the timbrel and dance;
praise Him with stringed instruments and flutes!
Praise Him with loud cymbals;
praise Him with high sounding cymbals!
Let everything that has breath praise the LORD.
PSALM 150:4-6

I praise you, glorious Father, with everything I
have that makes noise because your Word tells
me to make a joyful noise to you. Father, I clap
my hands, sing, and shuffle my feet, just because
I want to put everything I've got into worshiping
and praising you! I praise you with musical
instruments. If can't play one, I will bang two of my
kitchen pan lids together to sound like cymbals!
As long as I have breath, I'll continue to praise you!
Thank you for another wonderful month!

DECEMBER

Salvation

Salvation always begins with Jesus. We pray as you make these declarations this month, your salvation will become more real and personal to you than it ever has been before. May the Holy Spirit make you powerfully aware of the sacrifice of Jesus on your behalf as you rejoice in the God of your salvation!

I Believe in God

But as many as received Him,
to them He gave the right
to become children of God,
to those who believe in His name.
JOHN 1:12

I received Jesus, and you received me! Father, I thank you that because I accepted Jesus as my Savior and Lord, you gave me the right, privilege, and power to become your child. Because I believe in Jesus' name, I am restored to the fullness of your love, which is much greater than the love I have for my own children. I thank you and praise you that the gates of heaven have been opened to me because you sent your own Son to call me to my eternal inheritance of everlasting life! I love you and worship you because you don't care what I used to be; you only see me for what I am today, *your child*! Hallelujah, Father, how I praise you for that wonderful blessing!

I Am Born Again

Jesus answered him,
"Truly, truly, I say to you,
unless one is born again
he cannot see the kingdom of God."
JOHN 3:3, ESV

Thank you, Father, for sending your Son to show me the kingdom of heaven. I'm rejoicing because I've been born again of the Spirit and I praise you for making the truth so simple for me. Father, I love you because you didn't set up a complicated test I had to pass to get into your kingdom. You simply said I must be born again! Thank you, Father, for opening the windows of heaven to me! Thank you that because I have been born again, I will see your kingdom!

I Have Access to God

Jesus answered, "I am the way and the truth and the life. No one comes to the Father except through me."
JOHN 14:6, NIV

I praise you, Father, that your Word makes the way to salvation and eternal life so clear and uncompromisingly direct. Jesus said there was no other way to come to you except through Him. I praise you, Father, that I'm not wasting time searching for the way into heaven. I've knocked on the door and Jesus opened it for me! Thank you, Father, for the truth your Son brought me and for the life I have because He lives in me! I rejoice that Jesus is *the* way, *the* truth and *the* life! Thank you, Father! Thank you, Jesus!

I Am Restored to God

*For all have sinned
and fall short of the glory of God.*
ROMANS 3:23

Thank you, Father, that your Word tells me *all* have sinned and fall short of the glory of God. You didn't leave any room for arguing about whether I'm good enough to get into heaven the way I am. I praise you for making it clear that the law can't save me and that good works can't save me. Nothing I do on my own can save me. All have sinned, including me. Thank you, Father, that you have given me your Word so that I know what to do about my sins and be restored to you. Thank you, Jesus, that *all* I did to be spiritually born was to confess that I have sinned, ask God to forgive my sins, and ask you to come into my life. I was then born again!

God's Gift to Me Is Eternal Life

For the wages of sin is death,
but the gift of God is eternal life
in Christ Jesus our Lord.
ROMANS 6:23

Heavenly Father, I praise and thank you for the most precious gift on earth, the gift of salvation! I thank you for showing me that the wages of sin in my life are death. I didn't have your life flowing in me and I was doomed to be tormented in hell. Thank you, Father, for sending your wonderful Son, Jesus, to turn my life around! Thank you for snatching me out of the devil's hands and giving me a new life, overflowing with your blessings! Thank you for the beautiful gift of eternal life in your glorious kingdom through Jesus! Glory!

I Rejoice in My Salvation

For God so loved the world that He gave His only begotten Son, that whoever believes in Him should not perish but have everlasting life.

JOHN 3:16

I worship and praise you, Father, because you made the supreme sacrifice by sending your only Son to shed His blood on the cross just for me. Thank you, Father, for loving me so much that you were willing to let Jesus die that I might have eternal life. I can't thank or praise you enough for doing that. I rejoice that I believe in your Son, Jesus, who gave His life that I might die to my sins and live in you, to your everlasting glory! I praise you, Father! I praise you, Jesus!

I Am Cleansed

*If we confess our sins, He is faithful and just
to forgive us our sins and to cleanse us from
all unrighteousness.*

1 JOHN 1:9

Father, how I love you for your faithfulness to me!
I have sinned, but because I have freely admitted
and confessed my sins, I rejoice in the blessing of
your forgiveness. Thank you, Father, that you have
not only forgiven me, but you also have cleansed
me of all unrighteousness and buried my sins in
the deepest sea, never to be remembered again!
Hallelujah, Father, I'm clean! I'm walking in your
light and your endless love. I love you with all my
heart, soul, mind, and strength. Because you are
faithful to me, I'm being faithful to you. I'm blessed
by the joy of life I have in you! Glory! I rejoice that
you always do what your Word says!

Jesus Lives in My Heart

Behold, I stand at the door and knock. If anyone hears My voice and opens the door, I will come in to him and dine with him, and he with Me.

REVELATION 3:20

How I praise you, Jesus, for that day when you knocked on the door of my heart. I am so glad that I opened it and let you in. Jesus said if I heard His voice, He would come into me and dine with me. Because I heard Him, He is living in my heart right now! Thank you, Father, that I have the wonderful privilege of dining with Jesus, for I have never been so fully nourished in my whole life as I am now. I'm blessed because Jesus lives in me, I live in Him, and the river of your living water is flowing through me. Thank you, Jesus, for the marvelous things that have happened since I opened the door to *you*!

Jesus Redeemed Me from My Sin and Shame

For our sake he made him to be sin who knew no sin, so that in him we might become the righteousness of God.
2 CORINTHIANS 5:21

Thank you, Father, that Jesus, the sinless and spotless Lamb of God, was willing to take all the sin of the world upon His shoulders that I might receive your righteousness in Him. How I love you, Father, that you were willing to let your Son go through such a terrible ordeal for my sake. And how I love you, Jesus, because it didn't matter to you how horrible my sin was, you were willing to bear it on your innocent shoulders and take it to the cross for my salvation. Thank you for loving me more than I can possibly know in this life. I rejoice and give thanks that because I am dead to sin, I have everlasting life! Thank you for taking my sins, and in exchange, filling me up with God's goodness! I received the best end of the deal, and I love you *for* it!

I Confess Jesus is Lord!

If you confess with your mouth the Lord Jesus and believe in your heart that God has raised Him from the dead, you will be saved.

ROMANS 10:9

Father, I confess that *Jesus Christ is Lord*! I believe with all my heart, all my mind, all my strength, and all my soul that you raised Him from the dead to show me the way to everlasting life! Because Jesus lives, I live! Father, these words bless my tongue and lips as I confess them, and I thank you and praise you for the love that fills my heart right this minute. Thank you, Father, that I am a new person in Jesus Christ, and because I have believed, I am saved! Hallelujah!

I Am in God's Marvelous Light

For "everyone who calls on the name of the Lord will be saved."
ROMANS 10:13, ESV

Jesus, Jesus, Jesus! Heavenly Father, how I love to call upon the blessed name of Jesus. I know that because I have called upon the name of your Son, I am saved. Thank you that I am saved from darkness and called into your marvelous light so that I might know the truth you that you are light, and there is no darkness in you, at all!

Jesus Rescued Me

*For the Son of Man has come to seek
and to save that which was lost.*
LUKE 19:10

How I love you, Father! I didn't have to worry
and consider about how to find Jesus and get
His attention because you love me so much that
you sent Him to find me! I was a lost sheep and
even though Jesus has many sheep with Him in
His flock, I thank you that He came to rescue me
personally! Jesus knew exactly where to look for
me because there was no way for me to escape the
darkness and confusion of any sin on my own.
Because I'm found and saved, I'm blessed in your
love! I'm lifting my loved ones up to you who
are not yet saved. I thank you that Jesus hasn't
stopped seeking and saving the lost. I rejoice in
your promises that I am safe and secure in the
knowledge that as for me and my house, we will all
be saved!

I Have Been Made New

Therefore, if anyone is in Christ,
he is a new creation;
old things have passed away;
behold, all things have become new.
2 CORINTHIANS 5:17

Father, how I bless you that I am grafted into Jesus Christ. I am connected directly into Him, locked, fastened, attached, and joined to Him, exactly the same way a branch is connected to the vine. I've been born again! I am a new person because the life of Jesus pouring into my life has made me a fresh, new creation. Thank you, Father, that my old moral and spiritual condition is completely washed away by the blood of the Lamb. I praise you, Father, for giving me the blessing of new life! The old is gone; the new has come.

I'm Saved!

For with the heart one believes to righteousness,
and with the mouth confession is made to salvation.
ROMANS 10:10

I believe in Jesus with all my heart. I rejoice that because Jesus lives in my heart, I am made righteous through Him. Thank you, Father, that your righteousness is much, much more than the justice of this world. Your righteousness is perfect and without error. You are a wonderful, loving Father who cares for me. You have brought me into your perfect righteousness. Thank you, Father, for making salvation so simple in your Word, which says that if I believe in my heart and confess with my mouth, I am saved. I'm telling the whole world *I'm saved, I'm saved, I'm saved*! Hallelujah!

God's Plan Always Succeeds

Jesus gave his life for our sins, just as God our Father planned, in order to rescue us from this evil world in which we live.
GALATIANS 1:4, NLT

Father, I praise and thank you that Jesus was willing to give up His life to save, sanctify, and deliver me from the sin of this world. I rejoice and thank you for rescuing me from carnal greed, desire, sin, and corruption. I want to be about your business instead of the world's business. It really inspires me to know that when you made out your individual plan for my life, you placed many beautiful and magnificent things on my path. I praise you for that!

I Am Alive!

*And you He made alive, who were dead in trespasses
and sins, in which you once walked according to the
course of this world, according to the prince of the
power of the air, the spirit who now works in the sons
of disobedience.*
EPHESIANS 2:1–2

Father, how could you have ever loved me when I
was dead in the graveyard of sin? I walked in those
paths habitually, and yet you loved me enough to
stop me from following the fashion of this world. I
was under the temptations and pull of this present
day, following the prince of darkness. But you
grabbed me out of the devil's hands and claimed
me for your very own! How I praise you that even
though I was once rebellious, unbelieving, and
went against your purposes, you quickened my
spirit to see you and be born again! Thank you!

I Am Justified and Righteous

Being justified freely by His grace through the redemption that is in Christ Jesus, whom God set forth to be a propitiation by His blood, through faith, to demonstrate His righteousness, because in His forbearance God had passed over the sins that were previously committed.

ROMANS 3:24–25

Father, I fall so short of being an ideal person in your sight, and yet you declare me not guilty! I praise and thank you for your unmerited favor and mercy that you freely and graciously give to me. I thank you for the cleansing and life-giving sacrifice of the blood of your Son, Jesus, to save me from your judgment! How I bless you for passing right over all the things I did and forgiving them to give me eternal life! I shall praise you forever and forever!

I Am God's Workmanship

For we are His workmanship,
created in Christ Jesus for good works,
which God prepared beforehand
that we should walk in them.
EPHESIANS 2:10

Father, I praise you that I was created by you and born again in Jesus Christ! It doesn't matter what I look like to the world because I'm doing the job that you have always planned for me to do. Thank you, Father, that I am walking in your ways and living the good life according to the plan you had put into effect for me the moment I was born. Thank you, Father, you've given me my own special path in life! It's mine and no one else can walk it except me! I am your divine workmanship created for your glory. Hallelujah!

I Am Beholding God's Glory

And we all, with unveiled face, beholding the glory of the Lord, are being transformed into the same image from one degree of glory to another. For this comes from the Lord who is the Spirit.

2 CORINTHIANS 3:18, ESV

Father, I praise you for the miracle you did in my life! I love you for transforming my life as I behold the glory of the Lord through your Word, transforming and transfiguring me ever more into your very own image in ways that I don't have to understand, but simply accept. Father, I'm awed and thankful that you are changing me into ever increasing grace and into increasing degrees of glory through the Spirit. I rejoice at this mystery because I am being prepared to meet you! Glory!

I Receive God's Salvation

*Nor is there salvation in any other, for there is
no other name under heaven given among men
by which we must be saved.*

ACTS 4:12

I rejoice in you, Father, for you understand
everything and have determined your path of
salvation for the world. How I praise you that I
don't have to be a genius to know that there is
salvation in no other name except the name of
Jesus. There is no other way I could have been saved
except through that wonderful, majestic, powerful,
and magnificent name of Jesus! I believe in Jesus
and thank you for your marvelous gift. Hallelujah!

My Hunger is Satisfied

And Jesus said to them, "I am the bread of life.
He who comes to Me shall never hunger,
and he who believes in Me shall never thirst."

JOHN 6:35

Heavenly Father, I love the bread of life! I praise you that I will never hunger again because every day I feast spiritually on Jesus Christ, the Bread of Life. I praise you and worship you because I'm drinking at that fountain of living water. Thank you for giving me true food and drink, for in Jesus I am nourished to receive everlasting life and uplifted to live righteously in this world. Father, I love you for making such wonderful provisions for me.

God is the Author of Salvation

And having been perfected,
He became the author of eternal salvation
to all who obey Him.

HEBREWS 5:9

I thank you and love you, Father, because Jesus is the author and source of eternal salvation for each and every one of us who gives heed to your Word and obeys you. In spite of the pain you suffered by letting your only begotten Son die on the cross, you love me just as Jesus loved me by dying on that cross. I thank you because even if I'd been the only person in the world, Jesus would still have planned it this way. I love you, Father. I love you, Jesus. You are the author of eternal salvation for all who obey you.

God Loves Me and He Always Will

In this the love of God was manifested toward us, that God has sent His only begotten Son into the world, that we might live through Him. In this is love, not that we loved God, but that He loved us and sent His Son to be the propitiation for our sins.

1 JOHN 4:9–10

Father, your love is great! It prompted you to send your Son to be crucified, dead, and buried, until He rose again so that through Him, I might live, freed of the burdens of sin, redeemed in His blood, and restored to my inheritance of everlasting life in your heavenly kingdom. How I praise you that it was not my love for you, but your love for me that made all this possible. When there was nothing I could do to be raised from death in my sins, you sent your Son to bring me back to life. Father, I bow down before you in reverence and praise!

I Am Heaven-Bound

Assuredly, I say to you, unless you are converted and become as little children, you will by no means enter the kingdom of heaven.

MATTHEW 18:3

How I praise you, Father, that you open the gates of heaven to those who come to you like children with simple, uncomplicated faith. I love you, Father, for the teaching and instruction in your Word that lets me understand exactly what I must do to enter into the kingdom of heaven and abide in your glory. I come into your kingdom humbly and gratefully. Thank you, Father!

Glory to God in the Highest

"Today in the town of David a Savior has been born to you; he is the Messiah, the Lord. This will be a sign to you: You will find a baby wrapped in cloths and lying in a manger." Suddenly a great company of the heavenly host appeared with the angel, praising God and saying, "Glory to God in the highest heaven, and on earth peace to those on whom his favor rests."

LUKE 2:11–14, NIV

Father, today the world celebrates the birth of your Son. I praise you for the Good News that came out of Bethlehem over 2,000 years ago. I thank you that the same Good News is going out all over the world today, touching hearts and quickening spirits, just like it did long ago. Father, today I praise you for my salvation and I pray for the world. May kings and nations feel your priceless presence on this beautiful day of days!

I Have the Seal of God on Me

Do not labor for the food which perishes, but for the food which endures to everlasting life, which the Son of Man will give you, because God the Father has set His seal on Him.

JOHN 6:27

Father, this day after Christmas may we not look at the food that perishes or the things that pass away, but may we work and seek after the lasting food that continues until eternal life. Jesus, thank you for the wonderful gift of yourself. You provide abundant life and eternal life to me and my family. You are the gift that keeps on giving every day throughout the year. I give all my thanks and praise to you!

God Will Reign on the Earth

And they sang a new song, saying: "You are worthy to take the scroll, and to open its seals; for You were slain, and have redeemed us to God by Your blood out of every tribe and tongue and people and nation, and have made us kings and priests to our God; and we shall reign on the earth."

REVELATION 5:9–10

Heavenly Father, I offer praise and gratitude for letting me peek into the last days through your Word. Thank you, Father, for letting me know that my Lord Jesus Christ is worthy to take the book of the seven seals and to open those seals because He alone was slain and sacrificed. By Jesus' precious blood, He purchased people from every tribe, language, and nation to serve you. You've made us a royal race of priests to our God, and we shall reign over the entire earth as kings! Father, how I praise you that you included me and didn't leave me out of this wonderful world of your love.

I Will Pass from Death to Life

"Most assuredly, I say to you, he who hears My word and believes in Him who sent Me has everlasting life, and shall not come into judgment, but has passed from death into life."

JOHN 5:24

My ears are open to your Word, Father! I thank you for what Jesus said, and I hear it loud and clear. I believe, trust, and cling to you, relying wholly on you, and I now possess eternal life. I will never incur the sentence of judgment, and will not come under condemnation. I have already been passed over, out of death into life. I thank you that because I believe in you through Jesus, I have the blessing of eternal, everlasting, continual, ceaseless, timeless, infinite, unending, immortal, imperishable, and deathless life! Amen!

I Believe in Jesus!

Jesus said to her, "I am the resurrection and the life. He who believes in Me, though he may die, he shall live. And whoever lives and believes in Me shall never die. Do you believe this?"

JOHN 11:25–26

I will never die. What a glorious thought! Jesus, you raise the dead and give them life again. I bless you that even though this mortal body shall die, the real me shall live and never die. I thank you for that blessed hope. Father, I glorify you for sending Jesus to save me, and I will forever have faith in Him, cling to Him, and rely on Him until my very last mortal breath when I shall take on immortality and breathe a different kind of breath! I believe, I believe, I *believe* in you, Jesus.

I Will See God's Glory

*Then Jesus said, "Did I not tell you that if you believe,
you will see the glory of God?"*
JOHN 11:40, NIV

I want to see your glory, Father! Jesus, I want to see your glory! I wait with excitement and anticipation for that greatest day when you've promised I shall see the glory! Thank you for equipping me and perfecting me toward that day when I will at last stand before your throne and behold your glory and see you face to face. Father, how I long for that moment when I shall see your wonderful face! I'm excited about what it will be like to walk into your presence for the first time. I'm stirred up to see your glory and grace!

I Will Be Raised Up

No one can come to Me unless the Father who sent Me draws him; and I will raise him up at the last day.
JOHN 6:44

Father, I praise you for drawing me to you. As I celebrate the end of another year, I anticipate the day when I will be raised to spend eternity with you! Father, I bless you for having blessed me all this year. I praise you for your goodness, grace, mercy, divine health, peace, prosperity, loving kindness, abundance, your Word, your Holy Spirit, healing, the name of Jesus, strength, freedom from fear, blessings, faith, deliverance, and love. But most of all, I thank you for the assurance of my salvation and eternity with you.

Your Salvation Prayer

If you have never asked Jesus into your heart, please join me for this simple prayer:

Father, I want eternal life, but I know that I have done things that are not pleasing to you. I have sinned, and I ask for your forgiveness. Cleanse me of all unrighteousness. Jesus, I open the door to my heart and invite you to come in. Take control of my entire life, and make me the person you created me to be. I thank you, Jesus, for hearing my prayer and for coming into my heart as you promised. Fill me with your Spirit and empower me to be your witness in this world.

Now confess with your mouth these beautiful words: *I'm saved, I'm saved. By God's amazing grace, I'm saved!*